More Praise for *Engaging Emergence*

"To change or not to change, that is not the question! In a complex and fast-paced world, the only question is how to change creatively and successfully. Peggy Holman unlocks this complex challenge with a set of fundamental principles and practices. Follow them and your organization will flourish. Ignore them and it will eventually shrivel."
—**Henri Lipmanowicz, Board Chair, Plexus Institute, and former President, Merck**

"This book is simply brilliant. Peggy has done us all a great service—laying out clearly and effectively how to navigate through the chaos of our times into the emergent order that is the transformation we all seek and must deliver."
—**Lynne Twist, author of *The Soul of Money* and cofounder, The Pachamama Alliance**

"Not since *The Fifth Discipline* have I found a book on organizational learning that combines such powerful insights and useful practices."
—**Tracy Robinson, Executive Director, Seattle Center Foundation**

"Holman's work makes the compelling case that helping employees and stakeholders find a sense of ownership and optimism about the changes that engulf them is a key to successful transformations in any company or group. This book should be in the library of every manager who would like to help employees and stakeholders develop better mechanisms for coping with, and being optimistic about, change."
—**Chris Peck, Editor, *Memphis Commercial Appeal***

"Peggy Holman has tapped into a powerful evolutionary truth we can use today in our lives, our work, our world: disturbance tells us something new needs to surface. The more creatively we engage with disturbance, the more likely it will gift us its fruits. This book tells us how to garden disturbances to yield breakthroughs."
—**Tom Atlee, founder, Co-Intelligence Institute**

"Holman steps onto the shaky ground of the 21st century, finds meaning, and creates stability from our uncertainty. She builds our faith that coherence is out there somewhere, waiting to be discovered. Prepare to leap!"
—**Geoff Bellman, consultant and coauthor of *Extraordinary Groups***

"Thank you, Peggy, for disturbing us with this book. It is both provocative and confirming—providing a deeper unde_____ns and pointing to simple ways of enablin_____ g solutions."
—**Sandra Janoff, codirector, Future Sear**

"Peggy Holman is a theorist at the evolving edge of thought and application. ⌣⌣ puts clear language to the processes emerging around us in the field of change. We are grateful for her wide-ranging experience, networking, and wisdom."
—**Christina Baldwin and Ann Linnea, authors of *The Circle Way***

"Holman takes us on a journey into the heart of creativity at work. Her stories, illustrations, and key concepts provide guidance about how to invite, flow with, facilitate, and benefit from emergent processes. Read it and enjoy what emerges!"
—**Diana Whitney, PhD, coauthor of *Appreciative Leadership* and *The Power of Appreciative Inquiry***

"In this insightful and timely book, Peggy Holman helps us understand the deeper dynamics and principles at play in engaging emergence in constructive ways—enabling unexpected insights and collective intelligence to arise in our midst. I recommend it highly to anyone interested in new ways of working with groups and organizations."
—**Juanita Brown, cofounder, The World Café**

"If Margaret Wheatley's *Leadership and the New Science* opened our horizon to the new realities of contemporary leadership—uncertainty and complexity—this book turns these realities into practical approaches. I predict that for a long time to come the standard reply to the question 'But how can we deal with such immense complexity?' will be 'Read *Engaging Emergence*. It has the answers you are looking for.'"
—**Holger Nauheimer, creator and host of the Change Management Toolbook community**

"Peggy Holman's gem of a guidebook for midwifing collective intelligence and wise cocreativity is brilliant, timely, and well written. It is an indispensable map for successfully navigating humanity's rite of passage into maturity in the 21st century."
—**Michael Dowd, author of *Thank God for Evolution*, endorsed by six Nobel Prize winners**

"In a time of exponential change, 'change management' is quaint at best and probably doomed to fail. Our plans will be disrupted, our expectations turned on their heads. If disturbance is going to be our dance partner from now on, then the tools and principles in this book are the essential safety manual. They also point the way to a thrilling existence."
—**Vicki Robin, coauthor of *Your Money or Your Life***

"The field of emergence *is* emerging. It affects your life, your work, and the world, and it's been mostly invisible. Peggy's book gives you the distinctions to recognize it, the lived experience of it, and the practical levers to make it even more powerful and useful. This is *the* definitive tool on this subject."
—**Martin Rutte, coauthor of the *New York Times* bestseller *Chicken Soup for the Soul at Work* and Board Chair, The Centre for Spirituality and the Workplace**

ENGAGING EMERGENCE

Also by the Author

The Change Handbook: The Definitive Resource on Today's Best Methods for Engaging Whole Systems, Second Edition, co-edited with Tom Devane and Steven Cady, with more than 90 international contributors (Berrett-Koehler Publishers, 2007).

ENGAGING EMERGENCE

Turning Upheaval into Opportunity

PEGGY HOLMAN

BK®

Berrett–Koehler Publishers
San Francisco
a BK Business book

Berrett-Koehler Publishers, Inc.
235 Montgomery Street, Suite 650
San Francisco, CA 94104-2916
Tel: (415) 288-0260 Fax: (415) 362-2512 www.bkconnection.com

Ordering Information
Quantity sales. Special discounts are available on quantity purchases by corporations, associations, and others. For details, contact the "Special Sales Department" at the Berrett-Koehler address above.
Individual sales. Berrett-Koehler publications are available through most bookstores. They can also be ordered directly from Berrett-Koehler: Tel: (800) 929-2929; Fax: (802) 864-7626; www.bkconnection.com
Orders for college textbook/course adoption use. Please contact Berrett-Koehler: Tel: (800) 929-2929; Fax: (802) 864-7626.
Orders by U.S. trade bookstores and wholesalers. Please contact Ingram Publisher Services, Tel: (800) 509-4887; Fax: (800) 838-1149; E-mail: customer.service@ ingrampublisherservices.com; or visit www.ingrampublisherservices.com/Ordering for details about electronic ordering.

Berrett-Koehler and the BK logo are registered trademarks of Berrett-Koehler Publishers, Inc.

Printed in the United States of America

Berrett-Koehler books are printed on long-lasting acid-free paper. When it is available, we choose paper that has been manufactured by environmentally responsible processes. These may include using trees grown in sustainable forests, incorporating recycled paper, minimizing chlorine in bleaching, or recycling the energy produced at the paper mill.

Library of Congress Cataloging-in-Publication Data
Holman, Peggy, 1955–
    Engaging emergence : turning upheaval into opportunity / Peggy Holman. — 1st ed.
      p. cm.
    Includes bibliographical references.
    ISBN 978-1-60509-521-9 (pbk.)
    1. Organizational change. 2. Change (Psychology) 3. Emergence (Philosophy) I. Title.
    HD58.8.H656 2010
    658.4'06—dc22
                                    2010011164

First Edition
15 14 13 12 11   10 9 8 7 6 5 4 3 2

INTERIOR DESIGN: Laura Lind Design   ILLUSTRATOR: Steven Wright
COVER DESIGN: Barbara Haines   INDEXER: Katherine Stimson
COPYEDITOR: Elissa Rabellino   PROOFREADER: Annette Jarvie
BOOK PRODUCER: Linda Jupiter Productions

To my parents, Marvin and Ethel Kessler:
my father, who said, "use your head"
and my mother, who added, "follow your
heart."

CONTENTS

The real voyage of discovery consists
not in seeking new lands, but in seeing
with new eyes.

—Marcel Proust, *Remembrance of Things Past*

Albert Einstein famously observed, "No problem can be solved from the same level of consciousness that created it." Too often, we use tired change strategies to address complex problems, only to be frustrated by the results. Fortunately, emergence, a naturally occurring pattern of change, provides an alternative. Should we choose to work with it, emergence can take us to a new level of change-making competence. Simply put, emergence is order arising out of chaos.

This book is about working with emergent change. While others have explored what emergence is, this book also focuses on how to engage it. It prepares you to face disruptions and invite the people you work or live with to realize new possibilities together. To help you find your way, I describe a fundamental *pattern* of change and then offer *practices*, *principles*, and *questions* for engaging emergence.

As creative partners with emergence, we can ride its rapids into organizations, communities, and a world more alive, healthy, and engaging. The more we understand and work with emergence, the more we increase the possibility of outcomes such as government in which partisan differences lead to creative, breakthrough legislation rather than gridlock or compromises that no one likes.

Is This Book for You?

Are you facing upheaval, disturbance, dissonance, in some aspect of your work or life? If so, you're in good company with automakers, schoolteachers, bankers, electronics manufacturers, information technology professionals, journalists, and others who have lost jobs or experienced their industry faltering. Have you noticed the rich diversity of capabilities, cultures, and aspirations among us? Have you ever wondered how we can become more capable together than we are alone?

If you seek courage, hope, and faith despite struggle or collapse, this book offers a path to a brighter future.

- *Engaging Emergence* presents both compelling ideas and powerful actions for working with uncertainty, upheaval, dissonance, and change.

- It is for leaders, both formal and informal—managers, officials, community leaders, opinion leaders, change practitioners, activists, and change agents of all sorts—who face complex, important issues and seek creative alternatives for addressing them.

- It provides insight into the intellectual, emotional, physical, and spiritual landscapes that upheaval evokes in most of us, fostering compassion for ourselves and others.

- It offers a framework for understanding the larger forces at play that create the sense of disruption many of us are experiencing.

- It highlights individual and collective practices for working creatively with disruption.

- And it focuses on what is needed to renew ourselves and our systems wisely, conserving what endures as we embrace what wasn't possible before.

Whether you want a map of the territory, prefer focusing on what you can do, thrive on the unknown, or favor some combination, this book seeks to equip you for working well with shifts and disruptions. It provides practical perspectives on the dynamics of *emergent complexity*—increasing diversity, connectivity, interdependence, and interaction in the self-organized functioning of a system. It grounds this abstract but useful idea in stories about how emergence shows up in our lives. And it offers guidance for facing the unknown.

How My Perspective on Engaging Emergence Evolved

All change begins with disturbing the status quo. So my quest to understand emergence began, of course, with disturbance. It was 1989, and I managed software development for a cellular phone company. A major project was on the rocks. Because it touched virtually every department, lots of people had opinions about how to fix the situation. The company had hired an expert in Total Quality—a system of tools, processes, and practices that increase efficiency and effectiveness. He led a meeting attended by 30 people with a stake in the project. I was galvanized! In my 17 years of doing software projects, I had never seen so many perspectives coalesce so quickly into a clear, focused direction and plan of action. It was my first taste of what I now see as a fundamental pattern of change: interactions that disturb, differentiate, and cohere.

That meeting changed my life. I took responsibility for the Information Technology group's Total Quality effort and dove in to discover how to change the organization. We introduced new disciplines, such as process improvement, teamwork, and measurement. Over the next three years, the organization remade itself, becoming best in class by every measure. I thought I knew what I was doing. And I fell flat on my face. Disturbance, ever my ally, opened the door to deeper learning. In this case, it meant developing more compassion for myself and others.

In 1993, I took a role researching learning organizations, bringing what I discovered into U S WEST Communications—a 60,000-employee telephone company. That's when work got really interesting. I ran into these odd change processes: Appreciative Inquiry, Future Search, Bohm dialogue, and others that creatively engaged the people of a system in generating breakthroughs. In my first experience with one of these processes—Open Space Technology—I witnessed something I had thought impossible. I watched angry union technicians and company managers come together on solutions in which individuals and the organization both thrived. I was hooked.

I became part of an emerging field of practice that had no name. We practitioners began connecting with one another, sharing questions and stories via the new social technology: listservs. Vibrant worldwide communities of practice have coalesced around different change processes. Strong friendships and learning partners have been welcome byproducts.

Worn out by travel for U S WEST, I joined a forest products company as the director of quality for information technology. It provided fertile ground for experimenting with all I had learned, bringing struggles and successes along the way. After two and a half years, more equipped to face the unknown, I struck out on my own. It was daunting and exhilarating. *The Change Handbook: Group Methods for Shaping the Future* (Berrett-Koehler Publishers, 1999), coedited with Tom Devane, was an early achievement. Containing 18 methods for engaging whole systems, the book was my attempt to understand why these odd processes worked.

Following the book, that quest to understand continues through both practice and research. With businesses, nonprofits, government agencies, and communities, I use what I now call *emergent change processes*—methods that engage the diverse people of a system in focused yet open interactions. These methods catalyze unexpected and lasting shifts in perspective and behavior. I follow scientific literature on complexity, self-organization, chaos theory, and emergence. I have delved into spiritual practices, seeking answers to why these open-ended, nonlinear processes work. Doing so has increased my equanimity when facing disruption. As a result, I am better able to support others in engaging emergence. My own story has become more open-ended and nonlinear as my quest for uncovering the deeper patterns of these methods guides me.[1]

Because this search is not solo work, since 1993 I have been part of a loose cohort of friends I met through Open Space Technology—an emergent change process that invites people to self-organize around what they love in order to address complex, important issues. (See "About Emergent Change Processes" for a description of Open Space Technology.) Together, we have convened a number of Open Space conferences around ambitious social issues. For example, in 2003, "The Practice of Peace" brought 130 people from 26 countries, including such high-conflict areas as Northern Ireland, Nigeria, Burundi, Bosnia, and Haiti. Gatherings like this provided freedom for creative experiments that would not be likely in organizational settings. They also helped me to appreciate the communication and governance infrastructures that accelerate action in organizations once departmental boundaries are bridged.

After the shocking disturbance of a racially based shooting at a Jewish Community Center in Los Angeles in 1999, I joined with three journalists to cofound Journalism That Matters (JTM). I hoped my knowledge of emergent change processes could contribute to telling stories that served communities and democracies. This book draws many stories from JTM. The industry has been a learning lab for engaging emergence, making visible the agony and excitement in the death and rebirth of an industry.

My search for understanding the deeper patterns of emergent change processes took a step forward in 2004 when I was invited to a gathering on evolutionary emergence. Social philosopher Tom Atlee and "evolutionary evangelist" Michael Dowd (more on Michael and evolutionary evangelism in chapter 7) were planning an "Evolutionary

Salon." Scientists, spiritual leaders, and social activists were coming together to explore the implications of evolutionary emergence on human systems. Tom asked my help in hosting the meeting. With *emergence* in the title, how could I resist? Four Evolutionary Salons later, with funding from the W. K. Kellogg Foundation, Tom and I developed a model of evolution centering on the role of interaction.[2] It provided a missing link in my understanding of emergence that helped connect it with my change practice.

This book, which relates emergence to the practice of change, was seeded when Steven Cady, Tom Devane, and I published the second edition of *The Change Handbook* in 2007. Because the field has exploded, we included over 60 methodologies. The book's size disturbed me. It pointed toward something more fundamental that we didn't name. It mobilized me to finally address the question of why these processes work. My answers coalesced into this book. These processes work because they help us to engage emergence compassionately, creatively, and wisely.

As I look back on these last 20 years, I see how disturbance, differentiation, and coherence have shaped my life. I share these ideas with you in the hope that together, we can take them to scale. Just think of the possibilities if more of us knew how to bring together diverse, conflicted groups that creatively coalesce and generate innovative and wise outcomes!

ABOUT JOURNALISM THAT MATTERS

Since many Journalism That Matters (JTM) stories are in this book, here's a little background on the initiative.

Journalism That Matters generates innovations by convening, connecting, and inspiring the diverse pioneers who are shaping the emerging news and information ecology.

JTM's operating principles:

- Invite the diverse and evolving ecosystem of journalism. Include people from print, broadcast, and new media who are editors, reporters, bloggers, audience members, reformers, educators, students, and others.

- Create the space—a calm in the storm—for random encounters and conversations about what matters most.

- Work with the unknown, engaging with what's emerging in news and information in a democracy.

As of 2010, we have cohosted 14 gatherings bringing together more than a thousand people. The centerpiece of every gathering is one to two days using Open Space Technology for participants to set their own agenda.

Numerous breakthrough initiatives have been born at these gatherings. Legacy media people find hope, and new media people find fellowship and inspiration. A community of journalism pioneers is emerging, along with a growing culture of entrepreneurial journalism that serves the public good. Hope, inspiration, and excitement arise as participants catch a glimpse of a future in which they are part of the answer.

What's in the Book?

Engaging Emergence turns upheaval into a promising path for change. It provides a hopeful way to think about disturbance. It gives you practices, principles, and orienting questions for stepping into chaos.

The introduction describes a fundamental pattern of change, puts emergence in context with other forms of change, speaks to why engaging emergence matters, and identifies benefits of engaging emergence.

Making sense of emergence is the focus of part 1, "The Nature of Emergence." Chapter 1, "What Is Emergence?" defines the term, offers a history of emergence, and describes its characteristics. Because emergence isn't always sweetness and light, chapter 2, "What's the Catch?" identifies idiosyncrasies that make working with emergence challenging.

Getting to work is the focus of part 2, "Practices for Engaging Emergence." Chapter 3, "Step Up: Take Responsibility for What You Love," addresses a practice at the heart of engaging emergence. Given that emergence requires working effectively with disruption, chapter 4, "Prepare: Foster an Attitude for Engaging," covers three useful practices: embrace mystery, choose possibility, and follow life energy. Once you've prepared, chapter 5, "Host: Cultivate Conditions for Engaging," equips you to attract others by elaborating on the following practices for shaping productive, creative environments: focus intentions, welcome, and invite diversity. Chapter 6, "Step In: Practice Engaging," describes practices for interacting: inquire appreciatively, open, and reflect. Since the effects of emergence are not always immediately visible, chapter 7, "Iterate: Do It Again . . . and Again," looks at how emergence works with stability and incremental change over time. It considers the frequently asked question "How do we sustain the results?"

While the practices are useful on their own, they are part of a system for engaging emergence. Five principles—welcome disturbance, pioneer!, encourage random encounters, seek meaning, and simplify— are explored in part 3, "Principles for Engaging Emergence." These principles, each described in a chapter, came from marrying my work in emergent change processes with my study of emergence.

Part 4, "Three Questions for Engaging Emergence," introduces the last of this system. The questions map to the pattern of change mentioned earlier: disturb, differentiate, and cohere. They offer an orienting perspective for engaging emergence. Chapter 13, "How Do We Disrupt Coherence Compassionately?" speaks to why we might want to disrupt. It also clarifies the benefits of doing so compassionately.

To turn the way we usually think about creative engagement on its ear, chapter 14, "How Do We Engage Disruptions Creatively?" suggests acting from our passions. It contradicts what most of us have been taught about selfishness and service. Now that we have opened to creative engagement, chapter 15, "How Do We Renew Coherence Wisely?" reflects on what contributes to wisdom arising.

The practices, principles, and questions of parts 2 through 4 form a system for engaging emergence. The good news about systems: because they are interconnected parts, no matter where you begin, it leads to other aspects. The pieces reinforce each other, strengthening our overall understanding and capacity for engaging emergence.

With that understanding, "In Closing: What's Possible Now?" envisions what could emerge as increasing numbers of us work with emergent change.

The book ends with a "Summary of Key Ideas" and descriptions of the emergent change processes referenced in the book. Throughout the book, stories appear in a distinctive font.

As you read, consider how you might engage emergence to work with the disruptions you face. Together, we can turn upheaval into opportunities that can lead to innovative results with broad support and greater resilience in our families, neighborhoods, communities, organizations, and other social systems, such as health care, education, economics, and governance.

FROM CHAOS
TO COHERENCE

*Life is about not knowing, having to
change, taking the moment and making
the best of it without knowing what's
going to happen next.*

—Gilda Radner, *It's Always Something*

Change begins with disruption. Whether caused by something
small—a broken promise—or large—a hurricane sweeping
across a city—disturbance interrupts the status quo. We may find it
positive: a promotion, losing weight, a new baby. We may experience
it with dread: loss of a job, a contract, a life. No matter what the disruption, because it is disturbing, it can lead to change.

Disruption, disturbance, tension, upheaval, dissonance, chaos.
These conditions stress us. They often challenge our ability to work
together toward common goals. Some disruptions, like upheaval and
chaos, are more extreme, but they all stimulate change. And though
we usually relate to such situations negatively, one key shift to engaging emergence is developing a positive relationship with these sorts of

1

stressors. In fact, disrupting compassionately is a particularly effective approach.

Most of us avoid tension and disturbances. We attempt to plan them away, control them, or destroy them. Perhaps we hold in our anger because we don't want to cause a fuss. We feel a little more isolated as a result, but order is maintained. We learn to walk around these isolation zones, sometimes forgetting they exist. Yet they typically worsen with time. Alienation, rigidity, greed, intolerance, and inaction or violence grow. Such characteristics are present in many of our current crises.

What if tensions inspired curiosity? What if we knew how to express our anger, fear, or grief so that it contributed to something better? This introduction describes a fundamental pattern of change as a guide for working with disruption. It examines how disturbances surface useful differences that generate coherent order. It puts emergence in context with other forms of change to clarify when engaging emergence makes sense. It speaks to why engaging emergence matters. The introduction ends by naming benefits of engaging emergence.

A Pattern of Change

How does change happen? Whether it is human, cosmological, geological, or biological, some aspects of change are predictable. By understanding them, we are better equipped to work with them. Every system contains the following:

A DRIVE FOR COHERENCE—Relationship, unity, bonding, wholeness, coalescing—a coming together—convergence. Think of atoms forming molecules, people joining communities, or our longing to contribute to something larger than ourselves.

OCCASIONAL DISRUPTIONS—Interruptions to the status quo, unexpected actions—disturbance. Think of natural disasters, angry protesters, changes in work policies or laws.

A DRIVE FOR DIFFERENTIATION—Becoming separate, individual, distinct, unique—a breaking apart—divergence. Think of teenagers separating from parents to find their identity, a co-worker striking off to freelance, or our longing to be accepted for who we are.

These forces are constantly interacting, mutually influencing each other. Nature plays out this pattern over and over. For example, a new species appears, disrupts the existing ecosystem, sorts out who survives and who goes extinct, and ultimately arrives at a new coherent state. The same dynamics play out in human systems. A case in point: writing this book has been a constant ebb and flow of disruption, differentiation, and coherence.

The seeds of this book have been with me for years. The size of the second edition of *The Change Handbook* disturbed me. We were cataloging methodologies that were being created faster than we could document them. Something deeper was happening. Understanding that something mobilized me to write, hoping to see the different notions that surfaced. Eventually, the outline for the book you now hold coalesced. I was on a roll. I wrote to a schedule because the content was clear. Sometimes, my musings surfaced a useful distinction that found its way into the outline. The work was "steady as she goes."

The first draft was flowing out of me when I tripped. I was starting to write part 2. I had a headache. I couldn't concentrate. Forcing my way through left me exhausted, the material uninspired. Then it hit me: I faced disruption! I remembered the pattern of change. Treating my frustration with compassion, I acknowledged the disturbance and experimented with differences until something cohered. I realized there was no part 2. The book got simpler, and I got back to writing.

The resulting manuscript went to readers. I posted it on a blog. Feedback came from a variety of people, and I looked for distinctions and similarities among their responses. Themes coalesced. I planned my revisions, including adding stories and how-to tips; made an outline; and got to work. And the chapters got longer. Too long. The manuscript asserted itself and I was stuck. Worse, my editor found the organization confusing. This time, I got the message before the headache: welcome disturbance. I experimented with different strategies. What could I delete? Would breaking the material into more chapters eliminate the confusion? Could I use different visual presentations? As options differentiated themselves, I kept tuning in to what the manuscript itself was telling me. I listened for what wanted to emerge. With great editorial coaching, a breakthrough occurred: tell a nonlinear story in a linear way. And so I have.

———————

Mostly, the experience was a steady state of writing, reviewing, editing, and writing. Sometimes, distinctions led to incremental shifts—adding or removing a chapter. Occasionally, I threw up my hands when the manuscript's organization blew apart. Ultimately, it coalesced into a new, more coherent order. Steady state, incremental shifts, emergence. Understanding these different ways in which change happens equips us to work more effectively with disruption.

Forms of Change

Though all change begins with disruption, not all change is emergent. This book focuses on emergent change because it is least understood and we need more effective ways of working with it. Knowing how emergence fits with other forms of change provides perspective on why we are experiencing more and stronger disruptions. It also helps us to understand when engaging emergence makes sense. Emergence will happen whether or not we choose to engage with it. We increase the likelihood of less destructive experiences and more desirable outcomes by working with it. I characterize change in three forms:

STEADY STATE—Disturbance is handled within the existing situation. A minor fix is made, or the disruption is ignored or suppressed. Business as usual continues. For example, a speeder gets a ticket for driving too fast.

INCREMENTAL SHIFTS—Disruptions interrupt the status quo. We distinguish what the disturbance brings to the system and integrate changes. For example, a constitution is amended.

EMERGENCE—Occasional upheaval results when principles that keep a system orderly break down. Chaos sparks experiments. Current assumptions are clarified, and new possibilities surface. Ultimately, something dies and a new coherence arises that contains aspects of the old and the new but isn't either. For example, a revolution leads to a new form of governance.

Much of today's angst comes from treating all disruptions as if they fit a steady state scenario or, at worst, could be managed through incremental shifts. Economic upheaval, failing schools, increasing terrorism—all indicate larger forces in play.

The Consequences of Not Engaging Emergence

Most of our current strategies for handling disruptions work well to maintain a stable system or to manage incremental shifts. They are great for moving from where we are to a predetermined outcome. When the root causes of disturbance are more complex, often more emotionally charged, approaching them as if we were fixing a broken car can make the situation worse.

We maintain our sense of coherence by drawing boundaries, physical or psychological. We protect those inside our neighborhoods or organizations and keep "the other"—people we view as different from us—out. Fenced communities and security systems are growing around the world. Airplane travel and immigration are vastly more difficult because of the security we use to keep us safe.

Such methods are natural responses when our way of life seems threatened. They also isolate us. If someone holds a different view, we better not let him or her in. Bill Bishop's *The Big Sort* chronicles how people in the United States have sorted themselves into homogeneous communities over the past three decades. We choose neighborhoods, churches, and news shows most compatible with our beliefs.[1]

Even if we doubt our "tribe's" stand on an issue, many of us don't voice it for fear of being ostracized. We hold it in and feel more alone as a result. The outcome: we isolate ourselves based on differences and retreat into a posture of defensive rigidity. In contrast, engaging emergence uses our differences to bring us together, opening us to creative involvement.

So, increasing numbers of us face complex challenges and don't know how to solve them. Some of us feel stuck or overwhelmed by the accelerating urgency of the conflicts and challenges facing our organizations, communities, families, or even ourselves. Some of us have too many choices and neither the time nor the expertise to discern among them. Others of us see no choices at all. Familiar strategies lead to dead ends, leaving many seeking alternatives. Until we engage emergence, disruptions will continue erupting more and more destructively.

Consider an industry in upheaval: newspapers. Readership has been falling for decades. Even as newspaper executives acknowledge the radical shifts they need to make, they continue approaching change using the same old strategies. A 2008 article in *Editor and Publisher*, a time-honored industry journal, makes visible the tragic irony: while we may know we need to change, we don't always know how to do it.

"Turn and Face the Change—With Newspaper Industry in Crisis, 'Everything's on the Table,'" exhorted the article.[2] It ends, "If this is a seminal crisis, then we have to do some seminal thinking. And it really does have to be radical."

Yet the most innovative idea in the article was distinctly small bore: print less frequently. When the world economy faltered in 2009, the decline turned conundrum into catastrophe. About 15,000 newspaper people lost their jobs.[3] More than 100 papers closed their doors, including the 150-year-old *Rocky Mountain News*.[4] The decline was predictable, yet virtually every newspaper is choosing extinction over experimentation. In perhaps the ultimate irony, *Editor and Publisher* closed its doors in December 2009.

<hr>

Newspaper executives are not alone in struggling with how to approach change. In *Change or Die: The Three Keys to Change at Work and in Life*, Alan Deutschman quotes experts saying that the root cause of the health crisis hasn't changed for decades.[5] Yet the medical establishment can't figure out what to do about it. Individuals also resist change when facing disruption. Deutschman cites research into change-or-die scenarios for patients facing bypass surgery and other diseases that can be mitigated by lifestyle changes. Even when we know we must change, 90 percent of us won't alter our behavior to fit the new situation. We choose death over adaptation.[6]

The Other 10 Percent

In the spirit of turning upheaval into opportunity, what goes on in that 10 percent of cases where we choose adaptation? According to the researchers in Deutschman's book, people find fellowship that inspires, reframe disaster as possibility, and keep practicing. Rather than making incremental shifts, changing a habit here and there, they engage emergence. They redefine the fundamental assumptions that guide their image of themselves and their actions. And they don't do it alone.

In no particular order, the following table compares traditional thinking about change with ideas that support emergence. This list grew out of my work with emergent change processes. Understanding the differences can help us to make more informed choices about how we approach change.

Traditional Ideas about Change	Emerging Ideas about Change
Difference and dissonance as problems.	Diversity and dissonance as resources, with problems inviting exploration.
Restrain, resist disturbance.	Welcome and use disturbance in a creative dance with order.
Focus on the predictable, controllable.	Focus on the mysterious from a foundation of what we understand.
Ensure that there are no surprises.	Experiment; learn from surprises.
Focus on outcomes.	Focus on intentions; hold outcomes lightly.
Focus on the form and its stability.	Focus on intended function; work with forms as they arise and dissipate.
Hierarchy.	Networks containing natural, often fluid hierarchies.
Visionary leadership.	Shared, emergent, flexible leadership.
Top-down or bottom-up.	Multidirectional.
Work solo.	Work in community and solo, bringing our unique gifts.
Pay attention to the mainstream.	Pay attention to the dance between the mainstream and the margins.
Build/construct/manage.	Invite/open/support.
Follow the plan.	Follow the energy, using the plan as useful information.
Manufacture.	Midwife the birth of novelty and cultivate its development.
Assemble the parts.	Interactions among the parts form a novel whole.
Design processes.	Design processes and cultivate nutrient environments.
Handle logistics.	Cultivate welcoming conditions, including handling logistics.
Strive for sustainability.	Sustainability exists in a dance of dynamic tensions.
Incremental shifts.	Periodic leaps and incremental shifts.
Classical.	Classical skills that also support jazz and improvisation.
Declare/advocate.	Inquire/explore, using what is at the heart of our advocacy as a resource.

Changing Notions of Change

The next time you face disruption and don't know how to approach it, look at the left side of the table. If it reminds you of what you would ordinarily do, look at the right-hand counterpart. Perhaps you will find some new insights for handling your situation. If taking the approach on the right seems like a lot of effort, consider the reasons for doing so.

Why Does Engaging Emergence Matter?

Emergence—increasingly complex order self-organizing out of disorder—isn't just a metaphor for what we are experiencing. Complexity increases as more diversity, connectivity, interdependence, or interactions become part of a system. The disruptive shifts occurring in our current systems are signs that these characteristics are on the rise.

Today's unprecedented conditions could lead to chaos and collapse, but they also contain the seeds of renewal. We can choose to coalesce into a vibrant, inclusive society through creative interactions among diverse people facing seemingly intractable challenges. In many ways, this path is counterintuitive. It breaks with traditional thinking about change, including the ideas that it occurs top-down and that it follows an orderly plan, one step at a time.

We don't control emergence. Nor can we fully predict how it arises. It can be violent, overwhelming. Yet we can engage it confident that unexpected and valuable breakthroughs can occur. Working with emergence involves some unfamiliar notions:

EMBRACING MYSTERY—Asking questions in addition to stating answers.

FOLLOWING LIFE ENERGY—Using our intuition in addition to making plans.

CHOOSING POSSIBILITY—Attending to our dreams and aspirations, not just our goals and objectives.

Change is always happening. When it is emergent change, it seriously disrupts what's familiar. It behooves us to learn how to work with it creatively. Our survival in an increasingly unpredictable world is at stake. When change is treated as an opportunity, prospects for positive outcomes are all around us.

Emergent change processes have uncovered creative and productive ways to engage emergence. These methods have also surfaced some dependable outcomes from doing so.

Benefits of Engaging Emergence

Just because specific outcomes from emergence are unpredictable doesn't make working with emergence impossible. We benefit from engaging emergence in these ways:

INDIVIDUALLY, WE ARE STRETCHED AND REFRESHED—We feel more courageous and inspired to pursue what matters to us. With a myriad of new ideas, and confident of mentors, supporters, and fans, we act.

At an early Journalism That Matters gathering, a young woman, recently out of college, arrived with the seed of an idea: putting a human face on international reporting for U.S. audiences. At the meeting, she found support for the idea. Deeply experienced people coached her and gave her entrée to their contacts. Today, the Common Language Project is thriving, with multiple awards (www .clpmag.org).

NEW AND UNLIKELY PARTNERSHIPS FORM—When we connect with people whom we don't normally meet, sparks may fly. Creative conditions make room for our differences, fostering lively and productive interactions.

A reluctant veteran investigative reporter was teamed with a young digital journalist. They created a multimedia Web site for a story from a two-year investigation. Not only did the community embrace the story, but the veteran is pursuing more interactive projects. And the digital journalist is learning how to do investigative reporting.

BREAKTHROUGH PROJECTS SURFACE—Experiments are inspired by interactions among diverse people.

The Poynter Institute, an educational institution serving mainstream media, was seeking new directions because its traditional constituency was shrinking. As a cohost for a JTM gathering, Poynter had a number of staff participating. They listened broadly and deeply to the diverse people present. An idea emerged that builds on who they are and takes them into new territory: supporting the training needs of entrepreneurial journalists.

COMMUNITY IS STRENGTHENED—We discover kindred spirits among a diverse mix of strangers. Lasting connections form, and a sense of kinship grows. We realize that we share an intention—a purpose or calling guided by some deeper source of wisdom. Knowing that our work serves not just ourselves but a larger whole increases our confidence to act.

As a community blogger who attended a JTM conference put it, "I'm no longer alone. I've discovered people asking similar questions, aspiring to a similar future for journalism. Now I have friends I can bounce ideas off of, knowing we share a common cause."

THE CULTURE BEGINS TO CHANGE—With time and continued interaction, a new narrative of who we are takes shape.

When Journalism That Matters began, we hoped to discover new possibilities for a struggling field so that it could better serve democracy. As mainstream media, particularly newspapers, began failing, the work became more vital. We see an old story of journalism dying and provide a place for it to be mourned. We also see the glimmers of a new and vital story being born. In it, journalism is a conversation rather than a lecture. Stories inspire rather than discourage their audience. Journalism That Matters has become a vibrant and open conversational space where innovations emerge. New language, such as news ecology—the information exchange among the public, government, and institutions that can inform, inspire, engage, and activate—makes it easier to understand what's changing. People say, "I didn't know I could be effective without a big organization behind me. Now I do."

These experiences show that working with emergence can create great initiatives, the energy to act, a sense of community, and a greater sense of the whole—a collectively intelligent system at work.

As more people engage emergence, something fundamental changes about who we are, what we are doing, how we are with each other, and perhaps what it all means. In the process, we tear apart familiar and comfortable notions about how change works. We bring together unlikely bedfellows. For example, when Journalism That Matters hosted 44 mainstream journalists and media reformers in 2007, I watched them eye each other suspiciously as the gathering began. Once they realized that everyone cared about the role of journalism in a democracy, cooperation flourished.

The old story of change and how to do it, generally called *change management*, like many stories of our times no longer functions well. A new story is arising that works creatively with complexity, conflict, and upheaval. That story involves understanding more about emergence and what it can teach us about turning upheaval into opportunity. Later, we'll discuss practices, principles, questions, and what is possible as more and more of us engage emergence.

The theory and practice of change is too important to leave solely in the hands of experts. It is time to broadly develop the capacity to reenvision our organizations, our communities, and the systems where we live and work—health care, education, politics, economics, and more. Together, we can make it happen.

PART I

The Nature of Emergence

The only thing that makes life possible is permanent,
intolerable uncertainty: not knowing what comes next.

—Ursula K. LeGuin, *The Left Hand of Darkness*

Emergence is nature's way of changing. We see it all the time in its cousin, emergencies. What happens?

A disturbance interrupts ordinary life. In spite of natural responses, such as grief or fear or anger, people differentiate—take on different tasks. For example, in an earthquake, while many are immobilized, some care for the injured. Others look for food or water. A few care for the animals. Someone creates a "find your loved ones" site on the Internet. A handful blaze the trails and others follow. They see what's needed and bring their unique gifts to the situation. A new order begins to arise.

The pattern of change described in the introduction presented these aspects of emergent change:

- *Disruption* breaks apart the status quo.
- The system *differentiates*, surfacing innovations and distinctions among its parts.
- As different parts interact, a new, more complex *coherence* arises.

People often speak of a magical quality to emergence, in part because we can't predetermine specific outcomes. Emergence can't be manufactured. It often arises from individual and collective intuition—instinctive and unconscious knowing or sensing without depending on the rational mind. It is often fueled by strong emotions—excitement, longing, anger, fear, grief. And it rarely follows a logical, orderly path. It feels much more like a leap of faith.

Emergence is always happening. If we don't work with it, it will work us over. In human systems, it will likely show itself when strong emotions are ignored or suppressed for too long. Although emergence is natural, it isn't always positive, and it has a dark side. Erupting volcanoes, crashing meteorites, and wars have brought emergent change. For example, new species or cultures fill the void left by those made extinct. Even wars can leave exciting offspring of novel, higher-order

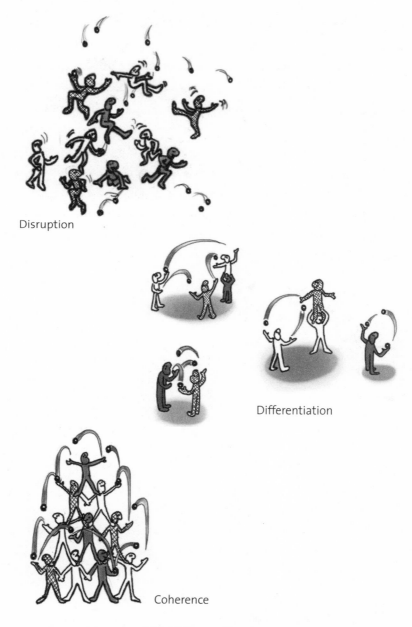

Disruption

Differentiation

Coherence

Disrupt—Differentiate—Cohere[1]

systems. The League of Nations and United Nations were unprecedented social innovations from their respective world wars.

Emergence seems disorderly because we can't discern meaningful patterns, just unpredictable interactions that make no sense. But order is accessible when diverse people facing intractable challenges uncover and implement ideas that none could have predicted or accomplished on their own. Emergence can't be forced—but it can be fostered.

The chapters in part 1 speak to what emergence is, how it works, and some catches to be aware of when engaging it. Making sense of a situation is tough when you're in the midst of the storm. Through understanding the nature of emergence, we can more effectively handle whatever changes and challenges come our way.

ONE

WHAT IS EMERGENCE?

*If you wish to make an apple pie
from scratch, you must first invent the
universe.*

—Carl Sagan, *Cosmos*

For most of us, the notion of emergence is tough to grasp because the concept is just entering our consciousness. When something new arises, we have no simple, shorthand language for it. The words we try seem like jargon. So we stumble with words, images, and analogies to communicate this whiff in the air that we can barely smell. We know it exists because something does not fit easily into what we already know.

Emergence disrupts, creates dissonance. We make sense of the disturbances that emergence creates partially through developing language that helps us to tease out useful distinctions. As the vocabulary to describe what is emerging becomes more familiar, our understanding increases. For example, *disturbance*, *disruption*, and *dissonance* are part of the language of engaging emergence. These terms are cousins, and I often use them interchangeably. *Disruption* is the most general of the three words. If something involves an emotional nuance, chances are that I call the disruption a *disturbance*. When conflict is involved or the disruption is particularly grating, with a lack of agreement or harmony, I will likely refer to its *dissonance*.

This chapter helps build a vocabulary we can all use by defining *emergence*. The chapter also provides a brief history of how our understanding of emergence has evolved. It offers some distinctions between strong and weak emergence and describes essential characteristics of emergence—what it looks like, how it behaves, and how it arises. The chapter ends by reflecting on the challenge of learning how to engage emergence.

Defining Emergence

In the preface, I defined *emergence* as simply as possible: order arising out of chaos. A more nuanced definition is higher-order complexity arising out of chaos in which novel, coherent structures coalesce through interactions among the diverse entities of a system. Emergence occurs when these interactions disrupt, causing the system to differentiate and ultimately coalesce into something novel.

Key elements of this definition are chaos and novelty. Chaos is random interactions among different entities in a given context. Think of people at a cocktail party. Chaos contains no clear patterns or rules of interaction. Make that a cocktail party in which no single culture prevails, so that no one is sure how close to stand to others, whether to make eye contact, or whether to use first or last names. Emergent order arises when a novel, more complex system forms. It often happens in an unexpected, almost magical leap. The cocktail party is actually a surprise party, and everyone knows where to hide and when to sing "Happy Birthday."

Emergence produces novel systems—coherent interactions among entities following basic principles. In his bestseller *Emergence*, science writer Steven Johnson puts it this way: "Agents residing on one scale start producing behavior that lies one scale above them: ants create colonies; urbanites create neighborhoods; simple pattern-recognition software learns how to recommend new books."[1] Emergence in human systems has produced new technologies, towns, democracy, and some would say consciousness—the capacity for self-reflection.

A Short History of Emergence

If we want to engage emergence, understanding its origins helps. Scientist Peter Corning offers a brilliant essay on emergence.[2] He brought a multitude of sources together to describe an evolution in perspectives. I have paraphrased some highlights:

- Emergence has gone in and out of favor since 1875. According to philosopher David Blitz, the term was coined by the pioneer psychologist G. H. Lewes, who wrote, "[T]here is a co-operation of things of unlike kinds. The emergent is unlike its components . . . and it cannot be reduced to their sum or their difference." By the 1920s, the ideas of emergence fell into disfavor under the onslaught of analysis. Analysis was seen as the best means to make sense of our world. In recent years, nonlinear mathematical tools have provided the means to model complex, dynamic interactions. This modeling capability has revived interest in emergence—how whole systems evolve.

- Emergence is intimately tied to studies of evolution. Herbert Spencer, an English philosopher and contemporary of Darwin's, described emergence as "an inherent, energy-driven trend in evolution toward new levels of organization." It described the sudden changes in evolution—the move from ocean to land, from ape to human.

Although evolutionary scientists have done much of the work, people from a variety of disciplines have also struggled to explain this common and mysterious experience. What enables an unexpected leap of understanding in a field of study or practice? In 1962, Thomas Kuhn contributed to our understanding by coining the term *paradigm shift* to describe a tradition-shattering change in the guiding assumptions of a scientific discipline.[3]

Then the Santa Fe Institute, a leader in defining the frontiers of complex systems research, took the work further. Engagingly told by Mitchell Waldrop in his book *Complexity*, the story of how the Santa Fe Institute was born reads like a great adventure.[4] In the mid-1980s, a hunch brought biologists, cosmologists, physicists, economists, and others to the Los Alamos National Laboratory to explore odd notions about complexity, adaptation, and upheavals at the edge of chaos.[5] Though their disciplines used different terms, they shared a common experience with this strange form of change. They were no longer alone with their questions. Others were exploring the same edges.

They gave this experience a name: *emergent complexity*, or *emergence* for short. While emergence has aspects of the familiar—Mom's nose, Dad's eyes—it is its own notion. It isn't just integrating old ideas with what's new. It is something more—and different. It is whole systems evolving over time. Single-cell organisms interact, and multicellular creatures emerge. Humans become self-conscious and track their own evolution.

In *Emergence*, Steven Johnson speaks of how our understanding of emergence has evolved.[6] In the initial phase, seekers grappled with ideas of self-organization without language to describe it. Without a coherent frame of reference, the ideas were like a magician's illusion: our attention was diverted to the familiar while the real action was happening unseen in front of our noses.

As language emerged—*complexity, self-organization, complex adaptive systems*—a second phase began. These terms focused our attention in new directions. People started coming together across disciplines to understand the nature of these patterns. The Santa Fe Institute was central to this phase.

During the 1990s, we entered a third phase, *applied emergence*, in which we "stopped analyzing emergence and started creating it."[7] In other words, we could see emergence occurring naturally in phenomena like anthills. And we started working with it—for example, developing software that recognizes music or helps us find mates.

This book is about creating conditions for applied emergence in our social systems. It aims to help us work with the dynamics of emergent complexity so that our intentions are realized as life-serving outcomes.

Distinctions Between Weak and Strong Emergence

Scientists distinguish two forms of emergence: weak and strong emergence. Understanding this distinction clears up some confusion. Predictable patterns of emergent phenomena, such as traffic flows and anthills, are examples of weak emergence. In contrast, strong emergence is experienced as upheaval. When disruptions dramatically change a system's form, as in revolutions and renaissances, strong emergence has occurred.

Weak emergence describes new properties arising in a system. A baby is wholly unique from its parents, yet is basically predictable in form. In weak emergence, rules or principles act as the authority, providing context for the system to function. In effect, they eliminate the need for someone in charge. Road systems are a simple example.

Strong emergence occurs when a novel form arises that was completely unpredictable. We could not have guessed its properties by understanding what came before. Nor can we trace its roots from its components or their interactions. We see stories on television. Yet we could not have predicted this form of storytelling from books.

As strong emergence occurs, the rules or assumptions that shape a system cease to be reliable. The system becomes chaotic. In our social systems, perhaps the situation is too complex for a traditional hierarchy to address it. Self-organizing responses to emergencies are an example. Such circumstances give emergence its reputation for unnerving leaps of faith.

Yet emergent systems increase order even in the absence of command and central control: useful things happen with no one in charge. Open systems extract information and order out of their environment. They bring coherence to increasingly complex forms. In emergent change processes, setting clear intentions, creating hospitable conditions, and inviting diverse people to connect does the work. Think of it as an extended cocktail party with a purpose.

Characteristics of Emergence

Although the conversation continues, scientists generally agree on these qualities of emergence:

RADICAL NOVELTY—At each level of complexity, entirely new properties appear (for example, from autocracy—rule by one person with unlimited power—to democracy, where people are the ultimate source of political power)

COHERENCE—A stable system of interactions (an elephant, a biosphere, an agreement)

WHOLENESS—Not just the sum of its parts, but also different and irreducible from its parts (humans are more than the composition of lots of cells)

DYNAMIC—Always in process, continuing to evolve (changes in transportation: walking, horse and buggy, autos, trains, buses, airplanes)

DOWNWARD CAUSATION—The system shaping the behavior of the parts (roads determine where we drive)

The phrase "The whole is greater than the sum of its parts" captures key aspects of these ideas. Birds flock, sand forms dunes, and individuals create societies. Each of these phrases names a related but distinct system. Each system is composed of, influenced by, but different from its mate: birds and flocks, sand and dunes, individuals and societies.

How Does Emergence Behave?

As with all change, emergence occurs when disruptions shape the interactions. In emergence, coherence breaks apart; differences surface and re-form in a novel system. The two most frequently cited dynamics:

NO ONE IS IN CHARGE—No conductor is orchestrating orderly activity (ecosystems, economic systems, activity in a city).

SIMPLE RULES ENGENDER COMPLEX BEHAVIOR—Randomness becomes coherent as individuals, each following a few basic principles or assumptions, interact with their neighbors (birds flock; traffic flows).

Twelve-step programs characterize these ideas at work. Most participants are fiercely independent people who are not there to follow someone in authority. Yet with the guidance offered through 12 statements, these programs are highly complex, worldwide organizations that have influenced the lives of millions.

No doubt the simplicity of these two dynamics may leave many senior executives and government agency heads skeptical. No one is in charge? Not likely. Isn't it interesting that the word *order* is a term for issuing instructions? What happens when orders come from the top? If they disrupt existing functions of the organization, sometimes it moves in novel and useful directions. And sometimes the orders produce entirely unexpected—emergent—outcomes that arise from within the system, bearing little resemblance to the orders given.

If managers say, "We're too complex for simple rules," chances are they're confusing *complicated* and *complex*. We often make things more complicated than necessary. Filling out a form in a bureaucracy

is a common example. Complexity is entirely different. Complexity
has elegance. It is, to paraphrase Einstein, as simple as possible but
not simpler.

Emergence is an energy-efficient approach to accomplishing complex tasks. Consider the different costs of handling conflict through
dialogue versus war. Negotiations among a handful of diplomats can
lead to breakthrough agreements for all involved. In contrast, armed
conflict involves thousands and generally produces results that work
for one party, along with loss of life and property for all involved.
Quite a different proposition in time, money, and life!

How Does Novelty Emerge?

Two key dynamics shape how novelty arises—how systems, including
us, learn and adapt. Increasingly complex and novel forms emerge from
interactions among autonomous, diverse agents, like us, through

- feedback among neighboring agents, and
- clustering as like finds like.

Feedback

Systems grow and self-regulate through feedback. Output from one
interaction influences the next interaction. We talk to a neighbor, we
share some of the discussion with friends, and suddenly everyone in
town knows that Sally married Harry.

Disruptions are feedback. They signal potential change. Most of
us focus on the symptoms, the visible outcomes of such signals. A fight
breaks out, and we concentrate on who is winning and losing. What
caused the fight? How else might it be resolved? We ask different questions when we pay attention to what's behind the feedback.

Feedback opens communication. It connects what's inside and
outside, at the top and bottom, across and within systems. It gives us
a chance to notice what is emerging and discern its meaning.

Systems theory uses feedback loops to help us map how interactions influence each other. It names two types of feedback loops: reinforcing and balancing loops.

Perhaps this is how the fight erupted: I speak my mind. It pushes your buttons; you get mad and push back. Even if I hadn't intended to irritate you, now I'm on the defensive. To protect myself, I attack you. And things escalate. In what is called a *reinforcing feedback loop*, output reinforces an action in the same general direction—sometimes toward more, sometimes toward less. Reinforcing loops are also called vicious or, when healthy, virtuous cycles.

Another form of feedback occurs through *balancing feedback loops*. Opposite forces counteract each other. Separation of powers among executive, legislative, and judiciary branches of government illustrates balancing loops. Each keeps the others in check. In healthy systems, those that continually learn and adapt, balancing loops periodically interrupt reinforcing loops, ending their perpetual growth. Without such checks we get global warming, economic meltdowns, and cancer.

Clustering

As we interact, feeding back to each other, like attracts like. Some of us bond around a shared characteristic. For example, we both like the same candidate for office. Over time, small groups with similar interests form. Perhaps parents advocate for a new style of school. With continued interaction, small groups become larger groups. Increasingly complex networks take shape when something binds them together. Parents, teachers, and small businesses unite to create new types of schools. At some point, a complex and stable cluster arises. It has unique properties unlike its individual elements. A national movement for charter schools takes off. Something novel emerges.

Humans are talented at pattern matching—clustering like with like. We even do it unconsciously. We see it indirectly in how towns and cities form. Asian districts exist in San Francisco, New York, and London. All of the auto dealerships are in the same part of town. As maps of the Internet are created, clusters of highly interconnected sites are appearing. We are experiencing emergence in process. Through our increasingly sophisticated technology, we can track complex networks forming. New tools show us the neural networks of the brain, the ecosystems of nature, and social structures in cultures. The ability to see complexity is reinvigorating interest in emergence. We can finally study complex patterns over time and space.

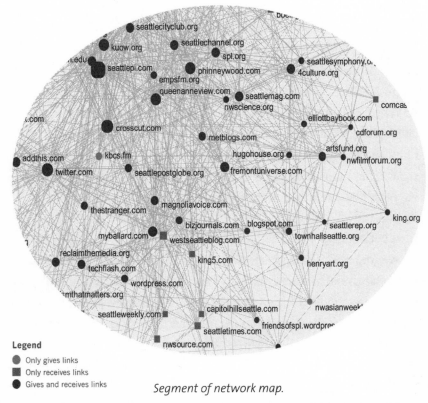

Legend

● Only gives links
■ Only receives links
● Gives and receives links

Segment of network map.

Pacific Northwest News Ecology—Extended Network[8]

Such tools make complex stories visible. For example, at a 2010 Journalism That Matters conference, a map of Northwest news and information Web sites caught the attention of an executive editor. He noticed the competition in the center of the map. He searched long and hard to locate his organization. A colleague explained that their antiquated technology caused the problem. No doubt, priorities changed when the executive returned to the office.

Learning How to Engage Emergence

The story of emergence is still young. We have struggled with its existence, described some of its properties, and given it a name. We are early in understanding what it means to social systems—organizations, communities, and sectors such as politics, health care, and education. We are just learning how to work with it to support positive changes and deep transformation.

In social systems, emergence can move us toward possibilities that serve enduring needs, intentions, and values. Forms can change, conserving essential truths while bringing forth innovations that weren't possible before. In journalism, traditional values of accuracy and transparency are making their way into the blogosphere, social network sites, and other emerging media.

Emergence is a process, continual and never-ending. It emphasizes interactions as much as it does the people or elements interacting. Most of us focus on what we can observe—the animal, the project outcome, the object. Emergence involves also paying attention to what is happening—the stranger arriving with different cultural assumptions that ripple through the organization or community.

Emergence is a product of interactions among diverse entities. Since interactions don't exist in a vacuum, the context also matters. That is why just bringing diverse people together won't necessarily lead to a promising outcome. Initial conditions set the context. How the invitation is issued, the quality of welcome, the questions posed, the physical space, all influence whether a fight breaks out or warm, unexpected partnerships form.

In truth, working with emergence can be a bit like befriending Kokopelli, a trickster of the ancient Pueblo peoples of the American Southwest, or his Norse counterpart, Loki. Working with mischievous spirits always has some catches.

TWO

WHAT'S THE CATCH?

Chaos is found in greatest abundance
wherever order is being sought. It
always defeats order, because it is better
organized.

—Terry Pratchett, *Interesting Times*

If emergence holds so much promise, why isn't it more widely embraced? First, we are just beginning to understand its dynamics so that we can successfully engage with them. More, working with emergence has a catch. In fact, it has several. The pages that follow describe six catches.

Catch 1: Getting Started Is a Leap of Faith

When breakthrough initiatives—the fruits of emergence—begin, there's nothing particularly spectacular about them. Quite the opposite. The seeds of most great ideas are misunderstood, dismissed, or discouraged by others. I heard author Peter Block summarize David Bornstein's *How to Change the World* by observing that successful social entrepreneuring projects begin small, slow, and underfunded.[1]

Beginnings are laden with self-doubt, false starts, dismissal as a crackpot, and other less-than-appealing experiences. Pioneering is not for the faint of heart. People blaze trails because of something so compelling that they feel they have no choice. Often, the reasons are obvious: a business collapses or a tsunami destroys the town. Sometimes, one person's inner drive carries an idea forward. The beginning of the "green jobs" movement highlights the leap of faith through which many initiatives are born. I heard Van Jones, human rights and clean-economy activist, tell this story in 2007, before his brief tenure in the Obama administration.

───────────

Jones's early years as a social justice activist had burned him out. As he put it, he had hit his head against the wall of injustice over and over. He broke, and the wall wasn't even dented. He needed to get away. He went on a spiritual retreat, something outside his normal experience. The retreat left its mark and brought him new friends from a different community. He found himself traveling between two worlds just 30 minutes apart. He lived in Oakland, California, where there wasn't a grocery store in the impoverished community. And he visited Marin County, where people worried about their carbon footprint while driving hybrid cars and eating organic foods. At some point, the dissonance coalesced into inspiration: green jobs. Retrofitting buildings to higher environmental standards—jobs that couldn't be taken offshore—married the employment needs of Oakland with the ecological sensibilities of Marin.

Jones brought the idea to the board of the organization he had founded, the Ella Baker Center for Human Rights. The support was underwhelming. No one "got" the idea. They had more pressing issues with policing and incarceration. Self-doubt was Jones's constant companion. He was responsible not just for himself, but also for the staff and supporters of the Ella Baker Center. Still, the call was strong and not to be ignored. With time, ideas like eco-capitalism and environmental justice started taking hold. Ultimately, the Oakland Green Jobs Corps emerged. According to the Ella Baker Center, which designed and championed the program, it is a "job-training and employment pipeline providing green pathways out of poverty."[2]

In 2007, a call came from Capitol Hill. Jones was invited to a meeting hosted by House Speaker Nancy Pelosi. Sitting at a table of 30 people, each with two minutes to share an idea, he needed to make his point fast and sharp. When his turn came, he had four words: green jobs for all. It stuck. At a press conference 15 minutes later, he stood behind Speaker Pelosi as she talked of a future with green jobs. The term has become a rallying cry for environmental jobs to lift people out of poverty. And it has gone around the world.

———————

Novel ideas are tough to communicate because they have no models. They start as seeds, intuitive hunches that are easy to ignore and challenging to embrace. When the calling is strong, even without knowing precisely what it is, we have no choice but to take the leap of faith and begin. As we experiment, experiences provide language. Language helps the notions take root and spread. A moment arrives, and a term like *green jobs* has meaning. Support grows, and eventually those outside perceive that the innovation is an overnight success.

Which brings us to the next catch.

Catch 2: Success Can Be a Hurdle

Since engaging emergence involves the unknown, it is risky. For many traditional leaders, success carries responsibility for the well-being of employees or community members. What if the risk fails?

In 2009, a journalism colleague struck a deal with a major news organization to develop software that supported a new business model. When the time to fund phase two arrived, the organization balked. It wanted more certainty before proceeding. For journalism organizations, certainty is years away. The implication of choosing inaction is to perpetuate the current decline, likely to be a fatal choice.

Yet their need for assurance is understandable, given the number of lives affected by their decisions. A publishing executive said to me, "We have plenty of ideas. There simply aren't the resources to pursue them all. We know we need to act. How do we choose among the options?"

Why did William Boeing "take one of the greatest risks in business history" on the 707 airplane in 1958?[3] What compelled Prosper Ndabishuriye, a Burundian minister, to look death in the face and unite Hutu and Tutsi youth to rebuild homes following the 1993 genocide in their country?[4]

A clue resides in crisis. When disturbance is loud enough, it helps crystallize what is critically important. Such was the case for a state agency that had lost the confidence of its constituency and faced life-altering funding cuts. As the agency's story shows, when we are unsure whether to step in, clarifying intentions catalyzes action.

━━━━━━━━

To solve the agency's crisis of confidence, the governor formed a blue ribbon commission. Among its recommendations: hire a new executive. She was charged with creating a strategic plan with broad-based public support. Funding was tied to the plan's success.

The director knew her future and that of her staff depended on a successful strategic plan. So did their work in the communities they served. She proposed to her board that they go well beyond a one-way public-input process. She wanted to host a statewide conversation.

As the board considered the idea, the members worried that individual agendas would prevail: rural versus urban, big versus small, east side versus west side. If they opened the way for individual expression, what would prevent the process from becoming a free-for-all, everyone battling it out for themselves?

At an early planning session, I worked with the board and staff to clarify the purpose of the planning process. We used Appreciative Inquiry—a process based in asking possibility-oriented questions that focus on what is working and what is possible to inspire collaborative and wise action. The board and staff delved into their own commitment to the field. They shared stories of how they had fallen in love with their work. By the time they were done, the focus of the planning process was clear. Even knowing that they didn't know exactly what would happen, they were convinced that engaging the public in a statewide conversation was the right process.

Ultimately, over a thousand people participated. They had two statewide and 18 community-based Open Space Technology sessions, an online forum, and a dedicated phone line. By the end of the first session, the board members were so thrilled with the spirit of cooperation that they forgot they had ever been afraid. The agency's constituency saw it as a respected convener and partner. Its funding was restored. Further, when a statewide budget crisis hit a year later, its constituents came to its aid. The agency retained adequate funding to do its work.

———————

Clear intentions can bridge the old world to the new with some assurance of landing on our feet or flying. While it won't eliminate risk, a clear, compelling purpose focuses our actions. And actions lead to outcomes, even if we don't always see them.

Catch 3: Outcomes Can Be Difficult to Recognize

At first it seems to be something we already know. When encountering novelty, our first impulse is to try to fit it into our existing frame of reference. Sometimes, seemingly minor shifts change fundamental assumptions of how things work. Years may pass before we appreciate the implications.

Consider the introduction of e-mail. It is just a quicker form of sending a note, right? Perhaps at first. Once we discovered how easy it was to send many-to-many messages, something new took shape. Suddenly, we could access more and different people. The volume of e-mail increased. With more messages coming in, how many of us have felt the weight of e-mail overload? As a 50-something, I grew up in an information-scarce world. My reading habits were shaped by the assumption that information was scarce, so I wanted more. With e-mail, blogging, Wikipedia, social networks, and other technologies, we now live in an information-abundant world. The assumptions of how to sort what to read are in flux. Yet I still feel obligated to read it all. I envy the people who assume that they'll be able to find all the information they need when they need it. They are wired to organize their reading differently.

With the rapid pace of technological change, many assumptions that guide daily life are changing. Even the forms evolve. We use computers rather than pen and paper. The underlying intention may well remain. Asking "What do we conserve that endures from the past?" and "What do we embrace that wasn't possible before?" can help us to navigate the change. Such was the case at a 2009 Journalism That Matters gathering that explored the question "What is our work in the new news ecology?" Participants uncovered something both ordinary and revolutionary. It seemed obvious, fitting existing assumptions. Yet the more they considered it, the more game-changing it became. Here's the story:

———

For two days, about 90 people from the whole system of journalism—editors, reporters, technologists, and others from print, broadcast, and new media—engaged in intense conversation about the future of journalism. On the last morning, people spent some time in quiet reflection. They looked for the patterns that mattered to their work. They shared stories in groups of three or four, listening for what had meaning to them all. They considered what endured that still held meaning. And they sought what was possible now that they wished to embrace. As a whole group, they identified the ideas that resonated most in the room. Among the insights, two were most heartily accepted:

- If it serves the public good, it's good.
- Journalism is now entrepreneurial.

No news there. Or was there? As I watched these seemingly obvious notions sink in, I could feel the wheels turning for many in the room. These simple statements contained important and liberating truths on the edge of journalism's rebirth. Legacy journalists, who thought they needed the name of their news organization behind them to be credible, realized that their voices counted even if they became independent reporters. New media people were affirmed in their wide-ranging experiments with new forms of serving communities and democracy. An ethic of service endured from the past. An entrepreneurial spirit was embraced as part of an emerging future.

At some point, it flips: what seems familiar and easily integrated into existing ways of thinking becomes a new organizing idea. Rather than fitting "serving the public good" into business models with pressures to produce content that doesn't matter, the journalism is liberated from its existing shackles. It is free to find new ways to survive. A vibrant, albeit chaotic, renaissance in journalism is under way as this simple realization that journalism is now entrepreneurial and serves the public good gains traction. What was outside the realm of imagination—entrepreneurial journalism—becomes part of the system.

With this realization, whole new forms appear. Technologies support communities in covering news and information that matters to them, which supports society-wide action. Entrepreneurial journalism uses new forms of expression to meet its core intention of serving the public more effectively than ever. A myriad of experiments are in process. For example, an idea born at a JTM event is applying crowd funding to journalism. At the Web site Spot.us (www.spot.us), people post story ideas and attract pledges for small amounts of funding. When sufficient funds are pledged, the money is collected and an investigation is launched.

When change is so radical that it seems ordinary, emergence is likely involved. Only in retrospect do we appreciate it as life changing.

Another reason why outcomes can be difficult to spot is that they are the cumulative result of many small changes. Certainly home runs happen, projects so spectacular that they can't be ignored. More often, seeing the effects of the work takes time. Marvin Weisbord and Sandra Janoff, creators of Future Search, developed a strategy to address this challenge. Future Search is a process in which the people in a system explore their past, present, and preferred future. They transform their capability for action and create policies, programs, and projects that many had considered impossible at the start. After a Future Search, Marv and Sandra advocate regular review meetings so that people reconnect and share their activities. Thus you are less likely to hear, "Well, not much has happened since the event. Though we did this thing in my department/neighborhood." When 30 or 50 people each name the little something they are doing and hear each other's stories, they realize that remarkable change is occurring. It energizes and amplifies everyone's work.

The nature of emergence involves occasional big, discontinuous leaps, usually creating major disruptions. Years of small, incremental changes follow. Shifts are integrated into a new context, such as entrepreneurial journalism. Ultimately, outcomes are visible. By bringing these patterns to consciousness, we can work with the elegance of change, its own rhythm and pace. We move with it toward new possibilities, even ones we never anticipated.

Catch 4: What's Most Important Is Likely Not on Our Radar Screen

Unexpected consequences are often the most vital. We tend to look at the projects initiated as a measure of success. Or, if we're looking over the longer term, what projects were successfully implemented. While these are important outcomes, the real treasures are often more subtle.

Over years of watching temporary communities form and disperse, I have observed an exciting trend. Emergent change processes create a context in which trust and friendship grow. Networks form around these communities of friends. Perhaps the gathering launches a few projects, but the network continues learning and experimenting. These networks of people are one of the treasures from engaging emergence.

With little or no seed money, the networks surrounding different emergent change practices—Future Search, Open Space, World Café, Art of Hosting, Appreciative Inquiry, Dynamic Facilitation—are growing. Thousands of practitioners around the world could be catalyzed into action should an intention of sufficient magnitude arise. In the meantime, they share stories and questions, mentoring and being mentored, researching and learning together.

How these networks have organized themselves to behave with collective intelligence holds great potential for understanding new organizational forms. What if we took seriously the idea that all systems are self-organizing? Just imagine our organizations managing themselves without guidance from above. They operate as an ebb and flow of network connections, regulated by an emergent collective intelligence. No one is in charge; everyone is in charge. Or each of us is doing what matters to us, coordinating with others as we go. Collectively, it adds up to a smoothly running venture. Of course, it does take some support and new ways of thinking, as I learned with some colleagues while on retreat.

A group of us gathered at Channel Rock, a retreat center on Cortes Island in British Columbia. Channel Rock was built to have a low-carbon footprint. It was designed to accommodate about 30 people, as long as they are conscious of their energy and water use. We were 10 people who put the systems supporting us seriously at risk. Why? We knew in the abstract that we should turn off lights and be mindful of our power use. In practice, we were creatures of habit. When our host saw that we were close to maxing out the water and energy systems, he took us on a tour of the power plant. We could see the gauges that told us the effect we were having on our environment. Until then, our power and water usage was an abstraction, the reality invisible to us. What an interesting insight: it is virtually impossible to understand our carbon footprint because the feedback is far removed from our actions.

As this story illustrates, we are babies when it comes to understanding how to use feedback well. Important outcomes may have nothing to do with what we focused on accomplishing. We may be receiving signals that we don't even know we need. In fact, disturbances are such signals. Learning how to work with emergence includes knowing that there are always unpredictable outcomes. The networks that form are an important gift in working with these unknowns. Even those who don't join in have something to contribute.

Catch 5: Not Everyone Makes the Trip

Most of us have experienced situations in which others have dived in, but we've chosen not to play. Perhaps the venue didn't suit us, the energy was wrong, or the circumstances weren't what we expected. Perhaps we go to a party that a friend talked us into attending, a workshop is different than advertised, or a church service has unfamiliar customs. Everyone around us is transported, but we are not moved. Sometimes we wonder if something is wrong with us. Or perhaps we think everyone else is running headlong into disaster, and holding back will vindicate us. Is it Wonderland, a magical mystery tour that changes us? Or is it Jonestown, with poison-laced Kool-Aid?[5]

In 2007, I cohosted a gathering in which a few people wondered if they had come to the wrong party. It offered some major lessons about disruption and compassion.

We—the conference organizers—brought together 83 storytellers of all stripes. We had writers, activists, futurists, visual artists, academics, musicians, documentary makers, advertising people, philanthropists, and others who shape the "story field"—the conscious and unconscious cultural narrative that defines how we collectively order our lives. The stories we tell, the clothes we wear, and the assumptions we make about wealth or leadership or community are all aspects of the story field. During the gathering, something disrupted just about everyone. Tensions surfaced that usually remain invisible: male/female, people of color/Caucasian, indigenous cultures/ Western culture, young/old. And yet—thanks to the process and hosting team—for most, the experience evoked curiosity rather than polarization. Deep, personal connections resulted. As differences surfaced, people spoke their angst, or fear, or pain. An indigenous woman expressed her anger about stolen stories when an anthropologist told a Maori story, intending it as a sacred offering. Her anger opened the door to a conversation about copyright, what different cultures hold sacred, and what that means cross-culturally. The compassion for and from both the storyteller and the woman objecting kept them engaged and connected with each other and those witnessing the exchange.

Most people left the conference understanding that the seemingly monolithic narrative of Western culture is actually many-storied and experienced differently based upon race, age, gender, subculture, class, and life experience. As one participant said:

> I came to Storyfield 2007 tracking capitalism and its ecological side effects. I expected to come away with ideas and inspiration about the transition to a sustainable human civilization. Once there, diversity and social justice issues captured my attention. What I came away with was mostly organized around tears—being frequently, unexpectedly moved to tears. Up to now, my attitude toward social justice issues could be summarized as—I'm all for it, but it is not my cause, not my passion. I have seen activist burnout, and sustainability seems like more than enough for me to work on.

> I got it that we can't get away with leaving the justice work for others to do. As long as the justice strand gets the least of our attention, it will continue to limit how deeply we can speak for sustainability. We become more effective in addressing sustainability by inviting diversity into the conversation, and doing our work around it.

This response was typical. Based on a post-conference survey, virtually every participant found the conference "mind- and heart-blowing." Many spoke of having come through the dissonance with a more complex understanding of their world and the relationships among the diverse people in it.

And yet, after the gathering, on the conference forum site, one man wrote:

> I don't get it. A group of 80-some adults are attempting to conduct a conference without structure and without facilitation. It is a disaster (in my humble opinion). But some participants seem to love it—as if there isn't enough chaos in daily life. I've been immersed in business for 30 years, where progress is easily measured and carefully planned. In a corporation, the difference between a bad meeting and a good meeting is palpable to everyone in the room. Give me a structured process where everyone knows what's going on, and everyone agrees to the ground rules.

To him, most of us had drunk the Kool-Aid. Yet his message seemed to be asking for help to understand what he had missed. His authenticity attracted a compassionate response from others.

People who take initiative often experience self-doubt. So do those who don't make the trip, like the man writing to the forum. Still, they play a critical role. They may be powerful voices for an initiative because their success in the current system attracts others who are changed by the experience. In the Old Testament story, Moses led the Israelites as they traveled in the desert for 40 years. During that time, the generation who experienced slavery died out. Moses never set foot in the Promised Land. I recall a Sunday school interpretation: he was of another time. The Promised Land wasn't open to him. But without him, no one would have made it to a new life. Which brings me to one last catch.

Catch 6: Death or Loss Is Usually Part of the Mix

Without death, there is no room for birth. Just think of the overcrowding if nothing or no one ever died! Death opens the way for something new to emerge. Without the death of stars, there would be no planets. Without the death of the dinosaurs, the small mammals that survived the meteor crash ending the reign of dinosaurs would never have opened the way for humans to emerge.

Perhaps fear of death, or more broadly, loss, is the biggest reason why we resist emergence. Loss brings grief. While death is ultimately a given, few of us choose to experience the emotional turmoil if we can avoid it. So we invent strategies that bury the root causes of disturbance, perhaps inadvertently setting up a system to die.

Just because death is essential to life doesn't make it easy. The seeds of the current collapse of the U.S. newspaper industry were visible long before it occurred. Readership had been declining since the late '40s. The rise of TV was considered the primary reason. To stem the tide, publishers listened principally to the needs of their primary revenue source: advertisers. By the 1970s and '80s, many newspapers made a strategic decision to focus on the readers most attractive to advertisers—people who could buy stuff. When our primary identity became consumers, the essential purpose of newspapers, to ensure that we had the information we needed as citizens, began to muddy. And circulation took a deeper dive.[6] Making choices that hasten our own demise is frighteningly easy if we close the door on disruptions, such as outside voices. While some may mourn, when a system ceases to meet the needs of the people it serves, its death opens the way for new alternatives. Many journalism alternatives are returning to the core purpose of journalism: providing the news and information we need to be free and self-governing.

As newspapers are discovering, denying disturbances leads to loss or death. Disruption has an interesting way of becoming more extreme when not adequately addressed. Ultimately, it forces our hand, and we acknowledge that business as usual is over. We mourn what is lost as best we can. We are well served to also let go of the operating rules from the past and admit that we don't know what to do. We can even ask for help.

We are in a special moment. Letting go of how things were opens the way for engaging emergence. What does it take to find the potential in the mess, to make it through the fear of loss or death? Part 2 offers some practices to help us face the challenge.

PART II

PRACTICES FOR ENGAGING EMERGENCE

I'm not afraid of storms, for I'm learning how to sail my ship.

—Louisa May Alcott, *Little Women*

A practice is a skill honed through study and experimentation. As every athlete or artist knows, practice takes discipline to develop both craft and artistry.

The practices for engaging emergence are rooted in skills of everyday conversation. Therefore, we all know something about them. They are our birthright.

The practices I highlight in this section consistently appear in the emergent change processes I use and those I have studied. When the issues are complex, the stakes are high, and emotions are right below the surface, these practices help us to engage.

Because working with emergence has nothing A-to-B-to-C about it, no one right way exists to use these practices. So part 2 is not an instruction manual. And while the practices won't tell you specifically what to do, they will tell you how you might approach different situations. They help us identify what to notice, what to explore, what to try. They are helpful hints for flying by the seat of our pants.

Just as scales prepare a musician and drills train an athlete, these practices equip us for the challenging conversations, the ones with disruption, difference, and the unknown. The practices are the conversational backbone for improvisation, enabling us to stay in the flow even if we don't know the specific path we're taking. Honing these conversational skills is how we engage emergence.

Occasionally I'll speak as if a practice were more solid and mapped out than it is. But I'll warn you now: don't believe it. We are at a growing edge of understanding how to engage emergence. Take what I say and give it a try. Experiment and share what you learn with as much humility (even when it's tinged with excitement) as you can muster. That's what I am doing my best to do.

I have organized the practices into five groups:

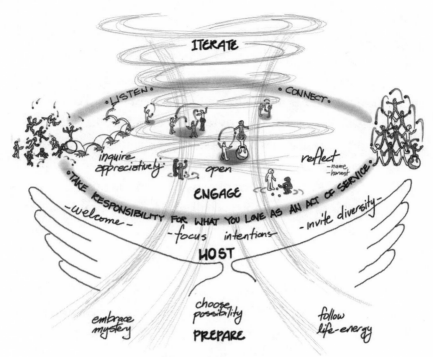

Practices for Engaging Emergence[1]

Step Up

Take responsibility for what you love as an act of service. This practice is a game-changing skill of engaging. It liberates our heart, mind, and spirit. It calls us to put our unique gifts to use for ourselves, for others, and for the systems that matter to us. The more this practice becomes our operating norm, the more innovation, joy, solidarity, generosity, and other qualities of well-being appear. The capacities for *listening* and *connecting* grow through this practice.

Prepare

The practices *embrace mystery, choose possibility,* and *follow life-energy* cultivate a composed state of mind, alert to aliveness and potential. They enable us to face whatever shows up with equanimity or even delight.

Host

Focus intentions and *welcome* are skills of being a good host. They create "containers"—hospitable spaces for working with whatever arises. They are the yin and yang of hosting. One emphasizes clear direction and purpose; the other ensures fertile ground for relationships and connection.

Invite diversity encourages us to look beyond our habitual definitions of who and what make up a system. It prepares us for innovation by increasing the likelihood of productive connections among people with different beliefs and operating assumptions. Inviting diversity is one of the most time-consuming, challenging, and critical activities of engaging emergence.

Step In

Inquire appreciatively is a second game-changing skill of engaging. The questions we ask determine the answers we uncover, shaping our experience, actions, and outcomes. Typically, the more positive the inquiry, the more life-affirming the outcome.

Open to the unknown. This practice is an act of faith. Once open, we can't go back. It may be the most countercultural practice of them all, requiring the courage to be vulnerable.

Reflect, *name*, and *harvest* can be sacred acts. They call forth that which previously didn't exist. The arts—music, movement, painting, sculpture, poetry, film—often enhance the effectiveness and reach of these practices.

Iterate

This practice reminds us of the never-ending nature of change. It takes time and perseverance to make its mark. Because our attention tends to get in caught in our routines, it is the most elusive of the practices.

● ● ●

Each practice is discussed and illustrated by a story. Tips for using the practice are also provided. So, let's begin by stepping up to engaging emergence by taking responsibility for what we love.

THREE

STEP UP: TAKE RESPONSIBILITY FOR WHAT YOU LOVE

When love is truly responsible, it is also truly free.

—Pope John Paul II, *Crossing the Threshold of Hope*

Taking responsibility for what you love, or, stated more fully, taking responsibility for what you love as *an act of service*, liberates us to act on our own passions—as long as they also benefit the greater good. Since we don't know which interactions among us make the difference, this practice points us to a promising source for guidance. I consider it the heart of the practices, because if we step up to it as a daily practice, it can change everything. It opens the way to situational leadership. We no longer need to wait for formal leaders or facilitators to declare an initiative or pose a good question. Any one of us can do so by taking responsibility for what we love as an act of service. When invited to do so, people consistently rise to the occasion. It may be messy, because most of us haven't been prepared to take responsibility for ourselves. Yet, over and over, people from all backgrounds develop the internal guidance to take responsible action. In doing so, they discover their connection to themselves, others, and the larger whole.

This chapter explores the notion of taking responsibility for what you love as an act of service. It also discusses two capacities we commonly develop from using this skill: connecting and listening. As with every practice in part 2, I'll discuss the practice, tell a story, and share some tips for application.

How can we use our differences and commonalities to make a difference?

By pursuing what matters to us individually, we often discover commonalities in our mutual needs and longings. Yet few of us follow our individual passions! Most of us were taught that pursuing what we love is selfish. So we set aside what makes us different and unique, and sacrifice ourselves for the common good. In practice, this choice often leads to unfulfilled, unhappy people who secretly take out their resentment on others. In contrast, when we embrace what we love, deeper meaning supersedes ego. We connect to something universal.

Just consider the power of this notion: paying attention to what we love. It frees us to interact in whatever way we see fit, to express our individuality fully. It challenges us to rise to the best in ourselves. It summons us to sense within, to bring our passions and abilities front and center, and to use them responsibly, come what may. When was the last time we were invited to do that? To do so takes both discerning what we love and having the self-love to bring it forward. These qualities help us to engage emergence.

By acting responsibly from a place of caring, we discover that both the needs of individuals and the needs of the collective are served. In fact, this discovery is a measure of success. When both individuals and the collective win, higher-order coherence is emerging. Though it may initially be disruptive, our uniqueness turns into creative contributions to the whole community. Another counterintuitive twist: withholding our individuality becomes the selfish act.

Many of us live with an unspoken belief that to belong, we must conform. Taking responsibility for what you love as an act of service can change this deeply ingrained cultural behavior. When we follow the energy of what matters to us, our distinctiveness contributes its creative potential. Time after time, unexpected and creative coherence emerges when people bring forth their unique voices. As this Journalism That Matters story shows, it also keeps the atmosphere hopping.

During the opening of a 2007 Journalism That Matters gathering in Washington, D.C., a 30-year veteran expressed his irritation with the state of "citizen journalism." Throughout the conference, fierce conversations raged between longtime journalists and newcomers. During the closing, that same veteran, with the same intensity, told us that the lively exchanges had uncovered the primary difference between pros and serious amateurs. The differences: (1) who gets paid, and (2) professionals cover stories, citizens share their stories.

One cranky journalist raised the bar on speaking authentically and passionately. He was determined to discover the difference that makes a difference between professionals and amateurs. He helped us all to understand a simple insight about changing relationships because he dared speak what was real for him. He helped everyone present experience the richness of creative engagement in its full voice.

Another lesson from this practice: When what is happening no longer interests us, leave. If we stay somewhere out of obligation, even when we're physically present, chances are we are absent in all other ways. Rather than our staying to be polite, if we have mentally checked out, this practice liberates us to go.

Taking responsibility for what you love as an act of service is a great life practice. The next time you notice yourself acting from obligation, test it out. Maybe you don't want to join the family dinner at Aunt Mabel's. What matters to you? Perhaps when you think about it, the sense of family is worth the questions about when you're going to get married. Or not. You choose. If you decide to go to Mabel's, it's guaranteed that your attitude will be different.

Beyond the personal, stewardship—tending to our collective needs—is a form of taking responsibility for what you love as an act of service. For example, if the river we grew up near is being polluted, it inspires us to act. Caring for the common good—whether the land, an organization, or relationships among us—is a key aspect of this practice.

I've struggled for a shorter phrase than *take responsibility for what you love as an act of service* and have given up for now. It is the essence of engaging, of taking initiative. Until we've got some practice with the idea, without the whole phrase as a reminder, we might stay in our seats waiting for someone else to act.

TIPS FOR TAKING RESPONSIBILITY FOR WHAT YOU LOVE AS AN ACT OF SERVICE

This simple, radical notion liberates us to act on what matters most. Be aware: it is contagious.

LISTEN TO INNER GUIDANCE. Ask yourself what matters to you. Discover, in essence, what brings you meaning. Consider the "shoulds" in your life. If they have no deeper meaning, let them go. Do what brings you joy, trusting that it serves the greater good.

STAND FOR WHAT MATTERS TO YOU. Learn how to disrupt productively. You can make your voice heard, even on unpopular matters, if you do it with compassion.

LEARN, CONTRIBUTE, HAVE FUN, OR LEAVE. Pay attention to your energy. If you have no juice for what is happening, do everyone a favor—be respectful and leave.

BE GENEROUS. When we give ourselves room to follow our passions, it awakens a sense of abundance in us. Honor the space that others need to grow more fully into themselves.

Most formal meeting facilitation structures participation. Everyone attends to the same issues at the same time. Perhaps circumstances exist where this is useful, but the most creative, energized, committed results occur when people follow their passions while being of service. It helps those with shared aspirations to discover each other. Nuggets of truth often hidden in anger, fear, grief, and joy arise as creative innovations. We find common cause, discover a deeper sense of self, a more human "other," and feel we are part of something greater.

Two capacities develop when we pursue what matters to us: listening and connecting.

Listen: Sense Broadly and Deeply; Witness with Self-Discipline

How do we more fully understand each other and our environment?

Listening cultivates a sense of the whole. It helps surface differences, connections, what we understand, what is mysterious. With practice, we can listen not just with our ears, but with all of our senses, including our heart and our intuition. Technologies make everything from bones to brainwaves available, amplifying our abilities to sense larger patterns.

Some structures, such as those provided by emergent change processes, make it easier to hear one another. Particularly in conflicted situations, when we know we will have a chance to speak about what matters to us, we are more generous in how we listen. Perhaps something others say can aid our work. In essence, useful structures provide space so that we open our hearts as well as our minds, knowing we have room to be heard.

Listening develops self-discipline. It enhances our ability to be with difference while maintaining common bonds. With practice, we learn to moderate our responses, increasing our capacity to witness without the need to judge, fix, blame, correct, applaud, cheer, shout, or say or do anything else. Unquestionably, times exist for all of these actions. Still, isn't it great to know that you can choose your response? The quality of our listening changes the conversation. Meaning arises that none of us could have found on our own.

Listen without judgment and with compassion. Most of us treat disagreements as a reason to debate, to convince the other person that we're right. Listening is sometimes used as a strategy for discovering arguments to undermine others rather than a means to understand them more fully. When I first discovered Circle Process, which elicits deep speaking and listening, I found an inquiry that served me well whenever I disagreed with something. I'd say, "That's an interesting perspective. Tell me more." The responses always took me deeper into another's world. The question also works well when I'm at odds with myself, uncovering deeper and sometimes contradictory assumptions that I hold.

One of my favorite stories about the transformative power of listening comes from my longtime learning partner, Mark Jones, who developed a practice he calls HSLing (hizzling)—*h*earing, *s*eeing, and *l*oving. He took the importance of listening to a new level in a life-threatening situation. Being willing to deeply listen made all the difference.

===

In the summer of 2001, I was living and working in the city of New Orleans. I spent every Saturday morning in a small, secluded park practicing classical guitar. I rarely saw anyone else. One Saturday morning, I heard aggressive voices echoing across the park. The voices got louder as six young white men emerged from the trees and walked toward me. I tracked them discreetly as I heard highly inflammatory racial epithets referring to me. They had apparently decided that I was an African-American. (I am.) They were verbalizing an intention to do me considerable bodily harm, if not commit downright murder.

As they got closer, I estimated their ages as 22 to 27. And they looked healthy. I put away my guitar and slowly stood up. (I'm tall and healthy myself.) When they were eight feet away, they began to fan out to surround me.

I quietly said, "Don't do that," and became very calm. My mind was processing two different streams of thought. One stream said that I needed to be prepared to die, to kill, or both. And the other said that there must be a creative, peaceful solution available from the insight that everyone wants and needs to be heard, seen, and loved.

The young men informed me that they belonged to a group of like-minded individuals who found my existence to be an affront to their personal sensitivities and to their god. They had been monitoring my appearance every Saturday for weeks and had determined that hurting me would provide an object lesson so that people would respect place and decorum. And they prepared to pounce.

I turned to face the "mouthiest" of the group. I had determined that he was the leader and the one that I would attack if I decided to respond aggressively. In a friendly and interested tone of voice, I asked him to tell me his personal story about why he wanted to harm me, how I was an affront to him. I told him that regardless of the outcome of the day, it was important to me to understand him, his life, his suffering, his frustrations, and his dreams.

For the next 45 minutes, he and his colleagues told me of their dreams and aspirations, values, beliefs, norms, proclamations, behaviors, essential conditioning, and experiences that had led them to this moment. It was a powerful and enriching dialogue. I was gifted with many insights about their conditions and conditioning that I had not been aware of. And they learned things about me that had them intensely curious and thoroughly amused. I asked them if they felt heard by me. They said yes and expressed appreciation for the opportunity. I asked them if they felt that they knew me. They said yes.

I then asked them, "Now what?" Six pairs of downcast eyes and one voice said that it was too bad that I had not shown up today. They might have killed me.

I told them that I was going to show up the next Saturday and wanted to know if they would kill me when I showed up. The leader said, "Yeah, we will kill you, but I don't want to. But we have to." Three of his colleagues blanched and said that they would not participate.

The leader asked me not to show up. I asked him, from what he understood of me, what was I going to do? He said I was going to show up. I asked him what he was going to do. He laughed and said he'd get back to me on that one.

I did show up at the park the next Saturday, and for most Saturdays until the weather precluded it. I never encountered that group of young men again. But I learned an important lesson about people needing first to be heard, in order to be seen. And that lesson probably saved my life.

Like all mammals, we have an innate need for belonging, being part of a coherent whole: a family, a workplace, a nation. As Mark's story poignantly shows, often fiercely holding on to an identity produces disturbances that divide us. One color oppressing another, nation against nation, religion versus religion. Even within a shared identity, we forget that it is not only possible but healthy to express anger or dismay to someone or something we love. Mark's story is a taste of what's possible. Unexpectedly creative encounters can lead to deeper bonds. They can bring about a more complex coherence, a *differentiated wholeness*. In other words, our distinctions contribute to a spirit of unity in which we are more than the sum of our parts.

TIPS FOR LISTENING

Listening, through all of our senses, informs us. It equips us to engage.

LISTEN WITHOUT JUDGMENT. By all means, notice your responses. Use them to understand the other person more fully. If, for example, you are shocked by what you hear, rather than reacting, ask a question that helps you to understand more fully.

USE MORE THAN YOUR EARS. We can listen through all of our senses—ears, eyes, touch, taste, smell, intuition, and technologies that expand our senses. We are remarkable instruments for taking in information, finding patterns, making meaning.

> **CHECK FOR UNDERSTANDING.** Repeat what you heard and ask if you heard correctly. At first, it can take many tries before another feels understood.
>
> **JOIN THE "HIZZLE" EXPERIMENT.** *Hear, see,* and *love* everyone, including yourself.

Listening often tunes us to another. It helps us to discover connections with each other and our environment.

Connect: Bridge Differences and Bond with Others

How do we link ourselves and our ideas with others similar to and different from ourselves?

Surprisingly similar ideas surface over and over when people with different perspectives creatively interact. We discover that what is most personally meaningful is universal. And more, we discover that we are not alone but part of some larger whole. As we experience this discovery, something shifts. "I" see myself as part of a larger "we." In this marriage of "I" and "we," something else emerges. We relate not just to each other but also to the whole. A social system—a community—emerges. It has its own identity, distinct from the individuals in it. And we are part of it. We share a common story, common intentions. Because we know in essence that we want the same things, our differences cease to be obstacles. They become creative pathways to unexpected innovations that contain what is vital to each of us and all of us. Our capacity and desire to listen to each other grows.

Here is a story of connecting. It was achieved through Future Search, a process that has the potential to transform an organization or community's capability for action in one meeting. With "the whole system in the room" (a cross-section of the organization or community), people generate a shared vision, an implementation plan, and a high commitment to act—all in less than three days. (See "About Emergent

Change Processes" for a description of Future Search.) Sandra Janoff, cocreator of Future Search, offers this example of what is possible when conditions foster connection, even in a traditional organization.

In a Future Search with the U.S. Federal Aviation Administration, a diverse slice of system users, regulators, and technology experts gathered to address the near-certainty of overcrowded airspace and potential gridlock in the skies. From past experiences in frustrating meetings, they came in with great cynicism.

Would they be willing to collaborate when changes in how air traffic was managed might cause pain to them all? As they worked together, they realized that the leadership for the future of aviation was in the room. Finally, one of the participants said, "We can't pass the buck anymore. We are the system. If we don't have the commitment and ownership, who does? We have to make the changes and share the pain."

They went on to tackle the "first-come, first-served" norm. They created a new system of accountability that would relieve daily congestion based on data from the whole system. Responsibility was shared by all.

As this story illustrates, when people discover that they *are* the system, everything changes. Not only can they act, but they are eager to do so, even when the work is challenging.

TIPS FOR CONNECTING

Connecting is at its best when we can express ourselves fully, knowing that it contributes to something larger.

BE YOURSELF. Though the idea is counterintuitive, our distinctions cohere into a larger whole. How can we discover that if we don't show up fully?

LISTEN FOR DEEPER MEANING. Often, disagreements show up in how to accomplish something. Pay attention to what's underneath, why it matters. Shared values frequently arise when we understand each other. We become willing to work through our differences. In fact, our differences become creative resources.

SEEK COMMON GROUND. Rather than focusing on differences, notice what brings us together. It provides a basis for collective action.

Taking responsibility for what we love as an act of service and its companions, listening and connecting, are fundamental life skills. They are a great foundation for all interactions. In particular, they set the stage for preparing to engage emergence.

FOUR

PREPARE: FOSTER AN ATTITUDE FOR ENGAGING

We are not what we know but what we are willing to learn.

—Mary Catherine Bateson, *Willing to Learn*

Emergence is rife with uncertainty. The more skilled we are in facing the unknown, the better able we are to engage emergence and to bring others with us.

How do we equip ourselves to engage disturbance?

Three practices—embracing mystery, choosing possibility, and following life energy—are particularly useful to cultivate. This chapter explores them.

Embrace Mystery: Seek the Gifts Hidden in What We Don't Know

What does it take to be receptive to the unknown?

Perhaps knowing that turmoil is a gateway to creativity and innovation provides a reason to open to the unfamiliar. Just as seeds root in rich, dark soil, so does emergent change require the darkness of the unknown. After all, if we know the outcome and how to create it, then by definition nothing unexpected can emerge. Even knowing its value, embracing mystery, being receptive to not knowing, takes courage. Buddhist nun Pema Chödrön speaks eloquently of this notion: "By not knowing, not hoping to know, and not acting like we know what's happening, we begin to access our inner strength."[1]

Mystery is essential to our well-being. Without the unknown, we have no learning. Without learning, our creative impulse goes unsatisfied. Without creativity, life loses its spark. We feel that loss in disease, disorder, violence, depression, and other unpleasant and unintended consequences.

We cannot avoid a fundamental truth no matter how thorough we are: holes always exist in wholeness. Some idea or group is always outside our frame of reference, mostly unseen. Because unknowns are always present, we are better served striving for excellence rather than perfection. The more we are at peace with the fact that the unknown is a given, the more we enter into it with a spirit of adventure.

While certainty has its merits, the more comfortable we are with uncertainty, the more we act with humility, taking ourselves—and others—with a compassionate grain of salt. Doing so prepares us to uncover useful distinctions in the dissonance.

If we aren't playing at the border between the known and unknown, we are standing in the way of our own evolution. Culturally, we celebrate perfection—perfect athletic performance, musical performance, total quality in production. It's a good thing we do. Virtuoso performances inspire us. And we sure don't want airplanes, bridges, and cars built any other way.

Still, mystery is a companion to perfection. It is equally essential. Yet it struggles for legitimacy. It lives at the margins, without a form or a name. Even the best inventions began as vague, mysterious inquiries. A scientist, talking about discoveries, said that all experiments begin by wandering through the forest, noticing all kinds of trees, and ultimately uncovering the nature of the forest itself. David

Gershon, author of *Empowerment*, calls this experience the "growing edge."[2]

Chris Innes of the National Institute of Corrections (NIC) found himself on that edge when he accepted a complex and ambitious task: transforming the corrections system in the United States. He embraced mystery, stepping boldly out of business as usual in a field traditionally resistant to change. His inspiring action took a traditional organization in a new, uncharted direction. He did so because he knew that "not knowing" was essential to accomplish his task.

===================

After researching strategies for changing social systems, Chris and his NIC colleagues chose to engage emergent change processes. They committed to travel unfamiliar territory. The decision was fraught with challenges from the hierarchy that authorized the work.

His board asked legitimate and traditional questions, like "What are you doing?" and "What do you expect to achieve?" With support from his management, Chris provided untraditional and courageous responses, saying, "We don't know. We are making it up as we go along. If we had the answers, why would we go to all this trouble?" While keeping the skeptics at bay, Chris is blazing a path that is taking shape as he and a diverse group working with him walk it.

In 2008, Chris brought together the Keystone Group, composed of diverse leaders from the field of corrections. Their role was to advise the NIC on how to transform the corrections system to be more just, humane, and efficient. Twenty people assembled for a weekend. They shared stories of why transforming the system mattered to them. Using Open Space Technology, they self-organized to explore the issues they cared about. People expressed their frustration with the existing system and began to envision new possibilities. A powerful question surfaced to guide their next steps: "How do we reduce the prison population by half while maintaining public safety, in eight years?"

No one predicted this focus. It arose out of interactions among deeply caring, knowledgeable, diverse individuals who came together in a nourishing environment around a question that mattered to them.

Chris, the NIC, and the Keystone Group continue their work. With their intentions clarified, mystery remains a central theme as they seek the means to accomplish their purpose.

═══════════

When sponsors, like Chris, experience an emergent change process for the first time, they often don't sleep well the last night before the gathering ends. They look for signs of the answers they seek in the day's work and find none. I can hear their unspoken thoughts: "Will I have wasted money and the time of a group of caring, committed people?" Yet at the end of the gathering, when unexpected coherence arises, as it did in the Keystone Group's question, they giddily exclaim, "I never could have imagined this great result!"

We don't need to be part of an emergent change process to embrace mystery. In truth, mystery surrounds us. Accepting its presence opens the way to engaging emergence.

TIPS FOR EMBRACING MYSTERY

Embracing mystery is less about doing and more about a state of being.

GET CURIOUS. Curiosity is a desire to know, to learn. Open to the unknown.

CLARIFY INTENTION. Why go to the trouble unless there is something you value? Intention—purpose—acts as a compass, setting direction while you travel in the wilderness.

INVITE OTHERS WHO CARE. People notice different aspects of a situation. With a shared intention, more eyes and ears, hearts and minds, increase the chances of uncovering the gems.

DEVELOP EQUANIMITY. Being calm in a storm increases the likelihood of surviving and bringing others with you. Personal disciplines—running, daily affirmations, practicing an art, regular meditation—are among the ways that people cultivate a capacity for facing the unknown.

Just as embracing mystery opens the way to discover hidden treasures, choosing possibility shines light in promising directions.

Choose Possibility: Call Forth "What Could Be"

What do we want more of?

Mark Twain once said, "You can't depend on your eyes when your imagination is out of focus."[3] When people tell us what they don't want, what they're against, it's a good time to ask compassionately, "What do you want?" If the question stumps them, perhaps they can describe a time when something worked.

Many societal cues encourage us to focus on what's broken, why we can't, what's wrong. We develop habits that reinforce these beliefs. We tell ourselves we're not good enough, smart enough, strong enough. Asking possibility-oriented questions shifts our attention and begins to break these habits. What do we want? What excites us, gives us meaning? What difference can we make? Such questions invite us to dream, to lift our spirits, to discover the gifts of our differences and come together around what inspires us. It takes commitment and practice to develop new habits of attention.

Geneva Overholser, director of the Annenberg School of Journalism at the University of Southern California, made that commitment. She introduced herself at a 2006 Journalism That Matters gathering, saying:

I had been depressed. A couple of years ago, I resolved to find hope. When you open yourself to possibility, you are willing to experience stuff you haven't experienced before.

Having made a choice, Geneva discovered plenty of examples to reinforce her new perspective. Her story makes it clear: whatever the circumstances, how we relate to our situation is up to us.

Choosing possibility isn't about ignoring problems. To do so simply causes them to show up elsewhere more destructively. Rather, our relationship to problems shifts when we view them through the lens of what we want to create.

Typically, we approach problems with two core questions: What's the problem? How do we fix it? This approach contains an implicit definition of what conditions are like when everything works. We focus on restoring the situation to a past state (or imagined past state). Think of Sisyphus, the mythological Greek king cursed to roll a huge boulder up a hill only to watch it roll back down, throughout eternity. His task echoes the energy of problem solving: hard work and discipline and often little joy. Even worse, the best we get is a return to some past state.

In contrast, when problems are used as a doorway to opportunity, three core questions typically guide us: What is working? What is possible? How do we create it? These questions mobilize us. Images of a brighter future draw us toward them. They fill a vacuum of possibility with joyous engagement. Ironically, the work may be harder than solving the problem. But it is infused with life energy—that invisible quality that attracts and enlivens—inspiring us to act.

TIPS FOR CHOOSING POSSIBILITY

Like embracing mystery, choosing possibility is a state of mind.

NOTICE YOUR HABITS OF THOUGHT AND LANGUAGE. Are they filled with deficits: "don't," "can't," "not," "isn't," "couldn't," "the problem is," etc.? Shift your focus from what you don't want to what you do want. •

REFRAME. Turn your thoughts and words around. If you're thinking, "I don't want that" or "The problem is that we aren't old/wise/creative/strong enough," ask yourself, "What do I want?" or "Given all that, what is possible?"

HAVE FUN WITH IT. Because we're surrounded by deficit language, I'm constantly turning it around in my mind. "State fails to pass budget." I ask, "What would it take to pass a budget that meets our needs?" When we're presented with possibilities, creative juices flow. As creative juices flow, we become more positive.

BE PATIENT. It took years to form current habits. Give yourself time to develop new ones.

RECRUIT YOUR FRIENDS AND COLLEAGUES. Practice is easier and more fun if others are also paying attention. Choosing possibility is a virtuous cycle. Doing it with others amplifies and accelerates the effect.

Follow Life Energy: Trust Deeper Sources of Direction

What guides us when we don't know?

Life energy is that elusive quality that attracts and enlivens us. Although invisible, it has vitality, a flow that we can sense. It animates all living organisms. It exists at the intersection of what we know and what we don't know, fueling us to make sense of mystery. Following the energy of an aspiration, bringing it to life, feeds us. Just as food fuels our bodies, life energy nourishes our soul. We know it is present because excitement, laughter, and joy break out. People are awake, alive, aware of their feelings. They are willing to be compassionate with themselves and others. In contrast, angst, pain, discontent are signs that life energy is stuck. Whether pain or joy, the feelings are present because someone cares. When we are prevented from following our passion, it can sour, becoming a source of disruption. Welcoming upheaval frees the energy so that it is available to engage.

My consulting colleague Tenneson Woolf shared a story of the contagious nature of life energy unleashed. He introduced the Canadian Union of Public Employees (CUPE) to Art of Hosting (AoH)—a global community of practitioners using integrated participative change processes, methods, maps, and planning tools to engage groups and teams in meaningful conversation, deliberate collaboration, and group-supported action for the common good. (See "About Emergent Change Processes" for a description of Art of Hosting and the other processes referenced below.) Tenneson tells the story of how creating hospitable conditions unleashes energy. It highlights the virtuous cycle that life energy creates.

———

In early 2008, CUPE labor educators were struggling to support members in rapidly changing workplaces aggravated by a rocky economy. We—four CUPE educators and three Art of Hosting practitioners—spent a day preparing for a four-day strategic planning session with 30 participants.

When the session began, we used a circle process check-in. People shared stories of the passion that brought them to their work. The unsticking began. In a common Art of Hosting pattern, from our check-in, we introduced models for working with chaos and complexity. Then participants dove into their projects using Open Space Technology to self-organize. The session ended with commitments to take the work out of the room: redesigning pension education programs, creating more green materials, creating a new culture of learning.

The work liberated participants, unleashing life energy! Satisfaction and joy flowed as they pursued their projects. One participant, who seemed preoccupied, told me that she was spending her mornings and evenings preparing for an upcoming workshop. I suggested she bring the work into the room and invite others to join her. In a 75-minute Open Space breakout session with six or seven of us, 90 percent of the concept came clear. She moved from concern to hope, from strain to lightness, from stuck to flowing.

The life energy from the session fueled a CUPE workshop on empowering local union leaders. That expanded to CUPE regions across Canada, into

CUPE coalition partners, into a Canadian Labour Congress learning circle, and then into the Canadian Auto Workers, the BC Government Employees Unions, and the Canadian Media Guild. All have taken up the mantle, redesigning their conferences and adopting participatory methods and leadership. CUPE staff and members are following life energy. They are delivering new programs and creating a new level of community.

When conditions welcome us to be authentic, joy appears and life energy flows. And flows. Seen in the context of tough realities, Tenneson's story grounds the ethereal notion of life energy and its ability to fuel change in practical reality.

TIPS FOR FOLLOWING LIFE ENERGY

Use all of your senses to work with the flow of forces that animate or deaden.

TUNE IN TO THE SIGNALS. Most of us depend heavily on our ears and eyes. We can hear and see laughter, tears, and other emotions. Yet we have many other ways of sensing what is happening. Our bodies, hearts, and minds provide information in different forms. Does our stomach clench? Do we feel warmhearted? Does something make rational or intuitive sense? Pay attention to where energy is stuck or flowing.

SUPPORT FLOW. If you wish to engage, participate fully, bringing all of your gifts. If not, get out of the way so that others can proceed. If you believe there is good reason not to proceed, disturb compassionately, supporting interactions that clear the way or bring closure.

TEND TO BOUNDARIES. Boundaries are often where life energy gets stuck. For example, organizational silos (departmental kingdoms), national borders, or how identity is defined create an inside and an outside. Boundaries are useful! They outline the edges of our systems. They just need attention. Permeable boundaries are more flexible, allowing mindful movement in and out. If we design the means to enter, exit, or change a system, then energy flows more fluidly. For example, if processes exist to improve a system, it channels life energy in life-serving directions.

These preparation practices help us to face whatever comes our way. We are better equipped to engage others, ready to host emergence.

FIVE

HOST: CULTIVATE CONDITIONS FOR ENGAGING

*As for the future, your task is not to
foresee it, but to enable it.*

—Antoine de Saint-Exupéry, *The Wisdom of
the Sands*

When disruptions are loud, situations are complex, and feelings run hot, we need change strategies up to the challenge. As appealing as it may be to "take charge," success is more likely with a "create conditions for something to emerge" strategy. The latter approach takes humility, curiosity, and the willingness to involve others. We cultivate these qualities by embracing mystery, choosing possibility, and following life energy. They prepare us to host others.

How do we steward what is arising among us?

Engaging emergence involves hosting, creating a "container" in which innovations can arise. A good container has a clear purpose, has a spirit of welcome, and invites the diversity of the system. Clear intentions provide direction and inspire a sense of purpose without defining

68

specific outcomes. Welcome conditions encourage authenticity and engagement. Diversity ensures that the unexpected is present.

This chapter discusses three hosting practices for cultivating productive containers: focusing intentions, welcoming, and inviting diversity.

Focus Intentions: Clarify Our Calling

What purpose moves us?

Pioneers are known for the clarity of their quests. Ponce de León sought the fountain of youth. Watson and Crick aspired to unlock the secrets of DNA. Single-minded determination strips away all but the essence of a calling. The strength of pioneers' questions fills them with the courage to act. Obstacles are simply challenges to overcome.

The work begins the moment we name an intention. It sets direction, inspires a sense of purpose, and sparks images of new possibilities. A myriad of books exist on defining purpose, creating a mission or a vision. Ultimately, we act from some inner calling that awakens both our head and our heart. A shared image of the future compels individual and collective actions congruent with our intent.

To uncover shared intentions, tune in. Listen to your own voice, that of others, and your environment. What are you sensing in and around you? What matters to you? As you get clear, invite others, particularly those different from you, to weigh in. Intention can deepen and clarify as others engage. Ask questions that draw out our deepest longings. Remember how emergence occurs as clusters form? When we listen to each other, our different callings can coalesce into a shared intention that serves us all.

Learn to steward shared intention by continually revisiting it. Particularly when we're feeling challenged, reconnecting with our intentions reorients us to our common work. Staying unattached to outcomes brings flexibility. It gives us access to many paths for accomplishing our intentions. Honor one another's individual callings while staying connected to what we share. Doing so increases the likelihood of finding answers that work for us all.

Disturbance, particularly crisis, can accelerate the quest for clear intentions. When the World Trade Center towers fell in New York on September 11, 2001, many people and initiatives clarified or reaffirmed their purpose. It galvanized Journalism That Matters. It helped us to dig deep into why each of us cared. And that coalesced into an intention that mattered to all of us.

When Journalism That Matters began in 2000, before it had a name, we were four people, each with different needs and motives. Our conversation had something to do with changing journalism. As we got to know each other, the aspects that mattered most began to surface: What is the nature of stories that serve the public good? How can journalism thrive as advertisers fall away? How will changes in technology affect the field?

This broad focus was sufficient to keep us talking. In fact, it was compelling enough that Chris Peck, one of the four and incoming president of the Associated Press Managing Editors (APME), invited us to host a day in Open Space at the APME national conference in October 2001.

As we prepared for that first conference, we struggled to name our session. Ultimately, we settled for "Saving Journalism." And then September 11 happened. The conference was just five weeks away.

The attacks on September 11 focused us on what was most important in our work. We met to finalize our plans a few weeks after that fateful day. Each of us spoke to our desires for what we would accomplish together. We realized the simple truth was that we were all committed to journalism that matters. We named not only a conference session. The initiative itself was born out of that naming. The name continues to guide us. It provides focus, attracts others who care, and constantly energizes us to reimagine journalism that matters in the midst of media's upheaval.

Clear intentions galvanize life energy. The clearer the image of what we wish to create, the more every choice we make reflects our focus. Although formal organizations can survive when intentions become diffuse, they are at their best when they have a clear, shared purpose. For efforts like Journalism That Matters—movements, networks, communities of practice, and informal initiatives—clear intentions are the glue that binds our diversity into a coherent whole, enabling individual and collective action that serves our intentions well.

TIPS FOR FOCUSING INTENTIONS

Clarity of purpose, an image of a desired future, orients us and galvanizes action.

CLEAR INTENTIONS DO THE FOLLOWING:

- Focus our work
- Touch our hearts
- Capture our imagination
- Attract participation
- Stretch the status quo, whispering at our aspirations

Ideally, they arise from a microcosm—a subgroup reflective of the system.

GET CLEAR ABOUT WHAT MATTERS TO YOU. Give yourself quiet space to reflect, to listen within. Some people meditate, some journal, some talk it through (without asking for or getting advice).

INVITE OTHERS TO NAME WHAT MATTERS TO THEM. Shared intentions set the stage for a virtuous cycle of trust and collaboration. As others get involved, welcome what they bring. Use differences and tensions creatively to enrich clarity and group coherence.

HOLD INTENTIONS CLEARLY BUT LIGHTLY. Distinguish between the qualities of desired outcomes and specific forms those outcomes take. Even if you have a specific outcome in mind, be open for whatever forms emerge. For example: we want journalism that matters.

It will likely involve many media, funding models, and participation from unexpected players.

CONTINUALLY REVISIT INTENTIONS. As situations change, as others get involved, intentions evolve. Hold them too rigidly and they lose life energy. When held lightly, evolving intentions are like layers of an onion. Each evolution comes closer to the core, to essential clarity.

Clear intention is laserlike, focusing our actions. It can move worlds. On its own, intention can lead to unfortunate practices. The genocide of indigenous populations when European explorers arrived in the Americas is ample warning of the risk. A spirit of welcome provides a moderating force. It is an essential ingredient for good hosting.

Welcome: Cultivate Hospitable Space

How do we cultivate conditions for the best possible outcomes? While clear intentions focus us, welcoming ensures that we are civil. It is far simpler to engage a diverse mix of people when they sense that they belong, right from the start.

Complexity scientists tell us that initial conditions are crucial in shaping what emerges.[1] Welcoming conditions make the difference between a screaming mob and a circle of peace. Creating containers that foster creative engagement sets up initial conditions for engaging emergence. You might call it the "vibe," the energy of a space or a group. Though we can't see it, we can sense it. Think of that small voice that informs you when you enter a place whether to relax or watch out.

The broader the diversity of people and perspectives, the deeper into a system you wish to go, the more important a healthy container is. Welcoming containers are grounded in clear, focused intentions; engage a relevant diversity of participants; and involve mindfully chosen practices and physical spaces that serve the purpose and people well.[2] We are cued both consciously and unconsciously about how much of ourselves to reveal, how deep we are willing to go together. When the environment supports us in expressing what might be considered disruptive in other settings, disturbances tend to show up as far less toxic. In welcoming spaces, people take charge of their situation, compelling facilitators to move out of the way and traditional leaders to contribute as one part of a larger system.

The work of cultivating a great container is a bit party host, a bit stage manager, and a bit den mother, and yet none of these. Like many relationally oriented skills, when practiced well, it is invisible. People feel welcome to bring all aspects of themselves present—not just their mind, but their feelings, their energy, their commitment. They know why they have come and what to expect—even when it is the unexpected. They can sense what they are welcome to say and do. A welcome space provides people with what they need to fully participate. It makes the difference between a room filled with silent hostility and one buzzing with hopeful anticipation.

Creating a container for the work is as important as setting a useful agenda. How do we make our intentions clear? Whom do we invite? What is welcome? What of our history needs to be shared? What of our aspirations? How about the physical space—what messages does it send? The questions are endless. All we can do is our best to discern the aspects that matter in any given situation. The good news: what we miss will show up as a disruption. By embracing it, we learn, adjust, and continue evolving.

A keynote talk I gave for an alumni conference of Seattle University's Organizational Systems Renewal program involved an experiment in cultivating welcoming space. The conference organizers and I conspired to learn something about the role that physical space plays in people's experience.

———————

The keynote theme was "the changing nature of change: an experiment in four movements." We divided the room into four quadrants, arranging the chairs differently in each section. One quadrant held a large circle. The second quadrant had café tables, each set for four people. The third quadrant was like an informal living room, with comfortable chairs, pillows, and throw rugs. The last quadrant was set in rows of chairs, like a classroom. I was in the center.

The talk itself became increasingly interactive. I began with a brief lecture. A question and answer period followed. We then moved into a conversational mode, with people discussing a common question in small groups, then as a whole group. Finally, we took a few silent moments for people to reflect on their experience and to discuss the role of the physical space in shaping it.

The people in the large circle loved being part of a whole. The café table participants reveled in the company of friends. The people in the living room were so comfortable lounging around, it wasn't clear that they had paid much attention to the keynote. Nor was it clear that they'd leave the space at break! The people in rows were grumpy. They felt constrained, isolated, and frustrated that they hadn't arrived sooner to get a "good" spot. People in the first three groups chose their seat according to the experience they wanted. The people sitting in rows were there because there were no other seats left.

Conference feedback was enthusiastic. The program director told me that several prospective students had enrolled because of their experience. A week later, I spoke with a student currently in the program. She said that most of the class was disappointed in the conference. As we explored the contrasting views, we realized that her classmates were expecting the intimate retreat experience of their weekend classes. The crowd, the fragmentation of people going their own ways, and even the tone of the keynote were at odds with their expectations.

––––––––––––

The conference experience highlighted both physical and subtle aspects of cultivating a spirit of welcome. The physical space cued participants on how to interact. The conversation with the student made it clear that knowing who is coming and what they expect matters. As an aside, a student joined the planning group for the following year's conference.

TIPS FOR WELCOMING

Pay attention to the physical, emotional, psychological, and spiritual messages you send.

SET CONTEXT. What do we need to be ready to engage? Knowing the purpose, why it matters, who is involved, is a good place to begin. Often, history is important. How did this get started? Who is hosting? Where does funding come from? Because so many elements can be part of the context, we won't always get it right. Prepare for that. Create the means for answering questions as they arise.

TEND TO THE SPACE. Be clear about the tone you wish to create. Create a physical space that says, "You belong," to the diverse people involved. Be sure that the room is clean. Perhaps a "Welcome" sign would help. Or nametags. Pay attention to the emotional space and the psychic space. For example, are both the head and the heart welcome? Since we can never predict all needs, put the means for adjusting in place.

IMAGINE YOURSELF ON THE RECEIVING END. What makes you feel welcome? Consider the diverse people—their roles, backgrounds, ages, and other factors—and stand in their shoes. What expectations do others have? If they are old, young, of another culture, of another discipline, what communicates hospitality?

SAY "YES AND . . . " In the heat of the moment, welcome what comes. Whether we like it or not, working with the unexpected as it arises increases the likelihood of a creative outcome.

Clear intention and a spirit of welcome are not enough to engage emergence. We need the people!

Invite the Diversity of the System

How can we include the true complexity of the situation?
Inviting diversity stretches us and broadens our understanding of our
world. Think of protesters outside the doors of power. What would
happen if, rather than shouting their messages, they were invited into
the room for an exploratory dialogue? While sometimes it takes violence or civil disobedience to be invited in, making space for different
perspectives in a system opens the way for creative engagement.

How do we decide whom to invite? The simple answer is: those
who care. Involve those with a stake in what occurs. Marv Weisbord
and Sandra Janoff, creators of Future Search, offer useful guidance
based on the principle of getting the whole system in the room. They
say, invite all who "ARE IN": those with *a*uthority, *r*esources, *e*xpertise, *i*nformation, and *n*eed.[3]

Inviting is the most time-consuming and often most challenging
aspect of hosting. It involves being receptive to unfamiliar perspectives, being willing to go to unfamiliar places, and cultivating relationships with people different from you.

My colleague Heather Tischbein took on this type of challenge
when she became the executive director for an environmental group
on the western slope of Colorado—the heart of oil and gas drilling in
the Rockies. She modeled the challenges and tenacity often required
when reaching out to the "other."

———————————

Heather was hired to change a combative activist group into an organization that could work creatively with energy companies and government to
bring viable solutions to the region. She spent a year reaching out to her conservative counterparts. She attended Chamber of Commerce meetings and
went to other places where she knew they would be, with little to show for it.
They didn't welcome her. The history of her organization told them that she
wasn't to be trusted. Still, she hung in, listening, asking questions, learning
about their perspective, while feeling pressure from her staff and board. They

couldn't figure out what she was doing. She was filled with doubt. Nothing in her environment affirmed her choices.

One day, the phone rang. It was one of her conservative adversaries calling to suggest a dialogue! What had happened? In Heather's words:

> I had introduced myself to the public relations person for one of the biggest energy companies doing business on the west slope at a community luncheon. I acknowledged that our organizations were considered to be enemies, but that my desire and intention was to make peace, not war. I hoped we might at least talk to one another. We could explore the possibility of finding common ground from which we could work together on behalf of the community, rather than perpetuate the polarized public conversation that was shredding the fabric of our community.
>
> She called me because no one from Western Colorado Congress had ever reached out to attempt a dialogue before. I was "different" than the "others" she'd met. She invited me to lunch with the public relations person of another big energy company. We talked about what it might look like to cohost a public dialogue on how energy resources could be developed compatibly with preserving and protecting the environment, public health, and legacy landscapes—what "we" all treasure about Colorado. It would be a dialogue that transcended or evolved beyond jobs versus the environment. Then she took me on a tour of a gas drilling rig—right into the heart of "enemy territory"!
>
> Some people assumed that her motivation was to coopt me or to create some good public relations smoke and mirrors. They took me to task for getting "sucked in" by her public relations expertise. I suggested that it couldn't possibly hurt to try to engage in diplomatic relations and to trust "good intention" until proven otherwise.

Although a change in the political climate prevented this dialogue, Heather and her counterpart continue to explore possibilities behind the scenes. Her story reflects a common challenge when the habitual response is to make "the other" wrong. Getting people together takes patience and practice. Heather continues living the spirit of invitation, holding an intention for creative engagement when there's an opening.

TIPS FOR INVITING DIVERSITY

Inviting the diversity of the system is a critical and challenging task for engaging emergence.

DEFINE WHO/WHAT MAKES UP THE SYSTEM. What functions, constituencies, or roles are involved? What mix of race, class, gender, geography, and generation is important? Are there nonhuman elements—for example, the environment or animals—that need to be present in some way?

GO WHERE THOSE YOU WANT TO PARTICIPATE LIVE AND WORK. If you wish to engage people from a different age, race, culture, etc., put yourself in their settings. Be humble. Listen. Learn. Reach out. They are more likely to join with you if they see that you are interested in a respectful partnership.

CREATE AN ORGANIZING GROUP THAT REFLECTS THE SYSTEM. The more a hosting group includes the mix of people you wish to engage, the more equipped you are to invite them to participate.

WORK WITH WHAT ARISES AMONG YOU. The organizing group is in the intensive course. The disturbances that exist in the system will show up in a diverse organizing team. Welcome the issues and work them through. Not only does it strengthen the group, but it prepares you for what's to come as you increase the scale and scope of your work.

Having created a focused, welcoming space with room for the diversity of the system, we are ready to step in and engage emergence.

SIX

STEP IN: PRACTICE ENGAGING

*Life is either a daring adventure or
nothing.*

—Helen Keller, *The Open Door*

We have prepared ourselves to engage and equipped ourselves to host, with a clear purpose and spirit of welcome. We have invited a diverse group to come together. We are poised to step in, confident that productive outcomes are possible.

How do we engage so that we achieve the best possible outcomes?

This chapter covers practices key to engaging emergence: inquiring appreciatively, opening, and reflecting. In addition to descriptions, stories, and tips on these practices, I offer two practices that amplify reflecting: naming and harvesting.

Inquire Appreciatively: Ask Bold Questions of Possibility

How do we inspire explorations that lead to positive action?

If your first impulse when facing disaster is to ask questions that surface images of a positive future, your chances of making it through upheaval increase. It kept psychiatrist Viktor Frankl alive, as he continually sought meaning even in a concentration camp during the Holocaust.[1]

Ambitious, possibility-oriented questions are attractors. They bring together diverse people who care. They disrupt, but do so by focusing on opportunities for something better, more meaningful. They help to create a welcoming environment, opening the way to discover what wants to emerge. A useful general question is "Given all that has happened, what is possible now?"

This question acknowledges the present situation without making it bad or wrong. And it focuses on the future, setting the stage for a productive inquiry. If we don't know the answer and are genuinely curious, we've got the beginnings of a great question. Here's a question about great questions: "How do we shape inquiries so compelling that they focus us on the best of what we can imagine, attract others, and connect us to realize what we most desire?"

Bold, affirmative questions bridge chaos and creativity. They mobilize change by helping us to envision our dreams and aspirations. Such positive images generate positive actions. Appreciative inquiries attract people from different aspects of a system to get involved. Tensions and conflict surface creatively when we bring together those who care to explore positive possibilities.

One creative idea that arose from Journalism That Matters is *possibility journalism*. In a sense, it codifies possibility as a journalistic principle. Think of it as a sixth W added to journalism's traditional who, what, when, where, why, and how. The sixth W: What's possible now?

Common Language Project cofounder and reporter Sarah Stuteville provides an example:

I was working on a story in Little Pakistan in Brooklyn, hearing about the experience of families who had members deported, mostly young men. I was talking to that community and to the non-Pakistani community. People felt strongly on different sides of the same issues. This was the first time that I asked, "What's possible now?" It may have come out of frustration, as it is hard to have conversations and not get anywhere. I threw my hands up and said, "OK, what is your ideal solution?" And everything changed. My contact began speaking of what coming to the U.S. had meant to Pakistanis prior to 9/11 and what he hoped it would someday be again.

Her partner Jessica Partnow offered a second story:

We—Sarah and I—were in the Middle East, talking with a Palestinian about frustrating, polarizing material. He kept repeating the same ideas over and over. So we asked that magic question: "Given what's happening, what's possible now?" It shifted the interview completely, as our contact began envisioning the situation in a completely new way, sharing his commitment to live a life with meaning in spite of the dangers.

As the Common Language Project people discovered, possibility-oriented questions don't avoid the pain of current reality; they help us to face it. The stories we tell ourselves shape the way we see the world. And that shapes our behavior. Asking "What's possible now?" follows life energy toward hopes and aspirations. While not denying harsh realities, it shifts a story's center of gravity from hopelessness and despair to possibility for a better future.

Great questions help us to face what we resist, creating room to be curious, to engage, contribute, and learn. Unapologetically affirmative inquiries orient us so that we can face the unknown with a strong spirit.

Picture the scene: Systems are failing, and people in traditional leadership roles are stumped. Discord fills the air. What has worked in the past no longer functions. Even if traditional leaders believe they are responsible for the rest of us, given the complexity of today's world, they have no chance of having all the answers. Leaders are set up for failure when ordinary people expect them to solve all the problems. Leaders who expect themselves to do so shoulder an impossible burden.

In truth, we've been acculturated to this trap, trained by school systems that set the expectation that we are supposed to know the answers. No wonder we resist complex situations in which we could not possibly, particularly on our own, have the answers!

Yet, when we face intractable issues, ultimately a turning point comes. We often experience that moment as a crisis and acknowledge that we do not know what to do. While it may initially feel like defeat, this moment is both terrifying and liberating. Into the chaos of not knowing, asking a question that invites others to join together in a search for answers provides a light in the darkness.

Bold, affirmative questions help us enter into mystery. They create some sense of safety. The unknown becomes a source of creativity where together we just might find some answers. When we reach the edge of known territory, ready to enter the unknown, a powerful inquiry orients us for the adventure ahead. It creates a safe haven so that when we step into terrain with angst or fear or despair or upheaval, we enter with our dreams and curiosity intact. We are able to stay in the fire to face whatever arises. We have paved the way for making the most of our differences by engaging disruption creatively.

TIPS FOR INQUIRING APPRECIATIVELY

Inquiring appreciatively is a life-changing skill. It helps us to find possibilities in any situation, no matter how challenging.

DEVELOP THE ART OF THE QUESTION. Practice asking questions that focus on possibilities. Here are some characteristics of great questions:

- They open us to possibilities.
- They are bold yet focused.

- They are attractive: diverse people can find themselves in them.

- They appeal to our head and our heart.

- They serve the individual and the collective.

   Some examples:

- What question, if answered, would make a difference in this situation?

- What can we do together that none of us could do alone?

- What could this team also be?

- What is most important?

- Given what has happened, what is possible now?

ASK QUESTIONS THAT INCREASE CLARITY. Positive images move us toward positive actions. Questions that help us to envision what we want help us to realize it.

PRACTICE TURNING DEFICIT INTO POSSIBILITY. In most ordinary conversations, people focus on what they can't do, what the problems are, what isn't possible. Such conversations provide an endless source for practicing the art of the question. When someone says, "The problem is x," ask, "What would it look like if it were working?" If someone says, "I can't do that," ask, "What would you like to do?"

RECRUIT OTHERS TO PRACTICE WITH YOU. You can have more fun and help each other grow into the habit of asking possibility-oriented questions. But watch out: it can be contagious. You might attract a crowd.

Appreciative questions provide a safe haven in which to explore disruptions, to open to the unknown.

Open: Be Receptive

How do we release assumptions of how things are to make space for new possibilities?

Opening happens in an instant. It is that moment when we let go of the beliefs that give our world order, and everything changes. We enter the heart of emergence. When Harry Potter stepped on the train platform to Hogwarts, he entered a world where the people in paintings talked and staircases moved at random.

While our situation may not be as radical as Harry's, opening sets us up for adventure. We no longer know what signals best organize our decisions and actions. Now is the time when all that pre-work—embracing mystery, choosing possibility, clarifying intentions, and so forth—pays dividends. We may not know the principles that organize our world, but at least we've prepared to face the unknown.

Ironically, "being open," "letting go," and "being receptive" are often judged as passive qualities. In practice, what could be more courageous than stepping in, with all of the energies—dissonant and resonant—that appear when difference is truly welcomed? Letting go of assumptions that have served us well is challenging. Yet without doing so, creativity has no space to flourish.

Facing significant change involves radically different beliefs and skills than handling daily routines. The landscape is filled with such uncertainty that virtually every effective action is counterintuitive. For example, consider doing business in an unfamiliar culture. Perhaps I look someone in the eye to communicate appreciation. Coming from a culture in which direct eye contact is inappropriate, the person interprets my look as aggression. We're off to a challenging start!

So set aside current assumptions. Be willing to say, "I don't know" and "We're making it up as we go along." These are today's forms of courage and strength. Stand on the shore of the known world and step into the creative waters of the unknown. It takes both exuberance and mindfulness. Pioneers thrive in this territory, exploring the differences, passions, perspectives, ideas, and dreams among us that make for creative engagement.

We open up once our intentions are clear. It makes sense. Why would we be willing to embrace disturbance without the promise of creative and innovative answers on the other side?

What do we want to accomplish? Is it a thriving organization or family? Or perhaps we envision a community that cares for itself. Whatever the focus, being receptive to disturbance is tough when we have been trained to *just do something*. We discover that finding our way is not a solo act. It demands more than "input." Wholeheartedly (and whole-mindedly) involve people from the many aspects of a system touched by disturbance.

Ironically, once we join others in the waters of difference, most of us find it exhilarating. We are freed from the "way things are," and creativity surfaces in abundance. Challenge and opportunity abound. Together, we revisit old ground with the benefit of each other's perceptions. We discover new and common ground. Engaging emergence can take on an almost mystical quality as chance interactions lead to unpredictable breakthroughs.

I had a challenging opportunity to open to the unknown when asked to host an Open Space Technology meeting for 1,800 street kids and 300 teachers in Bogotá, Colombia. It tested my faith in myself, in the Open Space community of practice, and in the Open Space process itself. It reminded me that opening, being receptive to what's present, involves risk. It takes a leap of faith. I am glad I made the leap.

I was going to Bogotá to teach a class. One of my contacts, Andrés Agudelo, invited me to work with him on a two-day Open Space meeting for 2,100 people. It was with a Catholic organization that prepares street kids, ages 14–22, for jobs. Only one Open Space meeting larger than 1,000 had ever been done. Still, I said yes.

When I arrived in Bogotá, we visited the site for the conference. It gave me reason to question my sanity. The room was designed to hold 1,000 people. As we considered alternatives, we realized that the courtyard leading to the room could accommodate 2,100. But we were in the rainy season. That's when I took the leap. I thought to myself, "I'm working with a religious organization. We're in God's hands."

The challenges continued. The organization received word that employers who provided jobs to the training program were threatening to quit. They said that kids were getting stoned and were stealing. The theme for our meeting took on a fear-based twist: from finding the best possible job opportunities, it became saving the jobs they had.

The oddest part is that I never panicked. Rain seemed inevitable, and 2,000 people would not fit in the room. The theme was the most fearful I have ever worked with. And one other item: I don't speak Spanish. Yet I was calm. I just knew it would work. Perhaps it was because I had a great partner in Andrés. And we were working with people who had handled huge crowds before. While they needed my expertise on Open Space, the kids, Andrés, and I were in good hands in every other way.

The day of the event dawned with blues skies and sunshine. I consider it a miracle. We convened in the courtyard. The event was spectacular, with two days of lively conversations that led to breakthroughs for the kids and their teachers.

Perhaps my calmness was due to the Open Space community of practice. Since 1996, its listserv has provided stories and advice for opening space. It gave me the confidence to do this work. I felt like I had a huge virtual consulting firm at my back. And for that I am deeply, deeply grateful.

When the unknowns are overwhelming but the rewards seem worth the risk, opening releases us into an adventure. Some of the most exhilarating and satisfying moments of our lives occur because we take that leap of faith. Such is the best of emergence.

TIPS FOR OPENING

Opening takes only a moment, but it may be the most courageous practice for engaging emergence.

BE CLEAR ABOUT INTENTIONS. Openness requires boundaries. Intentions clarify focus and set direction. Clarity of purpose creates boundaries that guide us from the inside out.

DO YOUR HOMEWORK; LET GO OF THE REST. Identify what matters and handle it. How we work with a crisis is a great teacher: we quickly discern what is critical and release everything else.

TRUST YOURSELF. We can study, prepare, and practice forever. Ultimately, safety, confidence, and the ability to rise to the occasion come from within. Decide what you need, handle it, and step in.

GO WITH FRIENDS. Challenges are best met with a diverse company of friends. Among you are more eyes, ears, hands, skills, and knowledge to respond. It is also more fun.

When we open to engaging, the practice of taking responsibility for what we love as an act of service moves into full swing. Whatever specific work we do, what matters to us is our guide. We're in the heart of creative engagement, discovering the differences that make a difference. While stumbling over disturbances, listening to ourselves and others, teasing out distinctions, connecting with what attracts us, and experimenting along the way, we ultimately notice what is coalescing. Reflecting helps us find our way to coherence on the other side of the chaos.

Reflect: Sense Patterns, Be a Mirror

What is arising now?

Reflecting helps meaning to coalesce. It is listening's mirror, making visible what we sense. It supports us in stepping out of the flow of activity. And it helps us to notice the larger patterns taking shape among us. By reflecting, we test whether we are ready to come together. Asking reflective questions helps us to perceive what is converging. What are we learning? What surprised us? What is meaningful? What "simple rules"—patterns, assumptions, principles—are surfacing? What can now be named? Buddhists say that you cannot predict enlightenment, but practicing meditation prepares the way. As both a solo and collective act, reflecting prepares us to notice what is shifting even as we experience it.

I use two complementary definitions for *reflecting*. They both help meaning to coalesce. The paragraph above describes reflection as contemplation, sensing patterns arising. This form of reflection involves actively seeking coherence. Reflection also means to be a mirror for others—to repeat their words or describe their feelings.

In this second form, reflecting is listening going deep, being a witness for another. Reflecting back the words and feelings of speakers helps them to hear themselves. It can get underneath ineffective expressions—shouting, whining, bullying—to the deeper longings buried in their angst. Supporting others to hear themselves clarifies the heart of their cry. Perhaps it helps them to realize what they wanted to express for the first time. Feeling fully heard frees them to listen to others.

Both forms of reflecting help us to notice our differences and stay connected. We discover the larger, more complex picture painted by our diverse views. That bigger picture is often an unexpected, coherent pattern that could not have arisen without deep expressions at the heart of our differences.

Reflection prepares the way for a new, wiser, higher-order coherence to emerge. What seems a contradiction—expressing individual desires when collective action is needed—is a pathway for coming together. My colleague DeAnna Martin offers a story of reflecting using Dynamic Facilitation, a process that helps individuals, groups, and large systems to address difficult, messy, or impossible-seeming issues. It does this by stimulating a heartfelt creative quality of thinking called *choice-creating*, where people seek win-win breakthroughs. (See "About Emergent Change Processes" for a description of the Dynamic Facilitation process.)

In the story, the power of reflecting comes through as participants engage their creativity, discover what they really want, and uncover possibilities they can pursue. The magic of solutions emerging when least expected is a highlight of DeAnna's story.

I facilitated a nine-member countywide parks and recreation volunteer advisory board that faced a familiar dilemma: increasing demand for services and decreasing sources of revenue. Among the board were a business owner, Little League coach, park volunteer, criminal justice system employee, retired professor, land developer, nonprofit director, community advocate, and mom. Also present was the board's staff-support person. They came from disparate cities—from the well-funded, liberal tourist destination to the poor, conservative rural town.

They began by looking at the complexity of their situation. What was the annual budget? Where did it come from? What were the annual expenses? Who cared about this? What did other agencies do about this issue? Two clear solutions emerged:

1. Like libraries, form a "junior taxing district," requiring voter approval; or

2. Acknowledge the cuts in revenue and cut back services.

A clear division surfaced over these options. Still, the participants shared a sense of despair and sadness in losing what all of them loved. I reflected—mirrored back—to them their proposed solutions and these feelings. In the process, I welcomed the dissonant voices, more like whines: "Passing a levy is too much work." "We don't even know what the people want."

With each reflection, the solutions and the issue evolved. The problem became, "How do we engage the public in figuring out what they want?" A new solution emerged:

3. Use fear to motivate the public. Put "We will be closing our most-loved park unless we can get more funding" on the front page of the local newspaper.

This solution wasn't quite right, either. What if no one cared about a park closing? The solution evolved yet again:

4. Put something in the newspaper and get the public's opinions about the proposed solutions: forming a junior taxing district or cutting programs.

Dynamic Facilitation helps groups to arrive at shared, unanimous outcomes. Three hours and 45 minutes into this four-hour meeting, the group appeared to know how it would proceed. A moment of silence invited a board member to speak: "If we vote to approve this plan, I cannot be on board. I care about our parks too much. I couldn't threaten to close one of them or do that to those who love them and use them as much as I do."

In my old facilitator mindset, with five minutes left, I would have ended there. Instead, I invited possibility. I asked, "Given that, what else might this group do?"

Someone spoke up: "We need to be united in moving forward. I want to find a better idea." Another board member hopped up and down in his seat. He had a novel approach:

5. We host meetings with potential partners like school districts, criminal justice agencies, sports leagues, youth programs, senior centers, and local elected officials. We share our situation and invite them to create partnership agreements to share the costs. We also host public meetings to share our situation and invite creative solutions.

With laughter and excitement in the air, all loved this idea. It meant they could discover what the public really wanted. It provided a financial solution that wouldn't cut programs or raise taxes. They quickly articulated the next steps. We were just five minutes over our allotted time, and the enthusiasm was palpable. Collectively letting go, engaging our curiosity, and using reflection to create shared meaning and action was worth it.

As DeAnna's story shows, when the way opens for expressing deeply felt differences, coherence is not far behind. Reflection makes space for our uniqueness to shine through, to name what matters to us.

I find reflecting one of the most magical and transformative aspects of engaging emergence. Reflecting sets a high bar. It challenges us, as Dynamic Facilitation teaches, to "take all sides" by valuing every contribution. It makes the rich tapestry of different ways of perceiving available to us, getting past triggers that usually block our hearing.

TIPS FOR REFLECTING

Reflection has two meanings. One meaning is to contemplate, to consider, actively seeking coherence. The other meaning is to be a mirror for another. Coherence arises in the process.

BE A MIRROR. Help others to feel heard. Repeat speakers' words to them. Describe their actions or expressions. Sense their feelings or deeper essence and tell them what you notice. Do it without judgment, with no strings attached, and without giving them advice.

LET GO OF THE NEED FOR IMMEDIATE ANSWERS. Make time to explore the depth and breadth of diverse perspectives without requiring a coherent response. Ideas need room to percolate. Relationships take time to form.

ASK QUESTIONS THAT SEEK CONVERGENCE. Reflective questions are different from questions that open us to face disturbances. Opening questions help us to discover distinctions by making space for wide-ranging exploration. For example, "What's possible now?" Reflective questions are useful once explorations are well under way. They focus on understanding coalescing themes and patterns. For example: What are we learning? What themes are surfacing that excite us? What is working well? What gifts have we received from this experience?

PAY ATTENTION TO THE TIMING. Checking for coherence too soon frustrates us. Waiting too long leads to fragmentation, the shadow of differentiation, in which we feel lost in our separateness. Casually ask a converging question—one that connects the dots. For example, what themes and patterns do you notice? What are we learning? What can we name now that wasn't possible before? If people aren't ready, the question is soon forgotten in the flow of interactions.

Reflection helps the wisdom that lives within and among us to emerge. When novelty surfaces that contains a bit of us all, yet is unique, we are at a special moment. We are ready to name something into being.

Name: Make Meaning

How do we call forth what is ripening?

Just as opening is a moment of letting go, naming is its counterpart, a moment of coming together. Difference coalesces, forming a novel whole. Naming involves a leap of insight, utterly unexpected and yet long awaited. At last, the finale of our midwifing emergence is at hand when we witness the birth of something new.

Our attention can shape what emerges. Giving something a name helps us to realize its potential. As such, naming something into being is a sacred act. When some scrappy British colonies named themselves the United States of America, a new form of governance was born that rippled throughout the world. Such is the power of names. They bring coherence to life.

Naming can seem like magic. Something unexpected suddenly appears. In practice, it is the culmination of all we have been doing. We inquired appreciatively into something that mattered to us, opened to explore what had heart and meaning, reflected on what ripened. Now we breathe life into our work with a word, a phrase, a name that distills meaning. With a name, a story can be told.

Years ago, I was on the faculty of a women's leadership program. The women had an assignment to do a service project together. They were given no more guidance. Their selection process and the nature of the project were up to them. At the time, I was living with a question of how collective decisions are made. Watching this group do its work taught me about naming something into being.

═══════════

Over several weeks, the women identified possible selection criteria for their service project. They researched and shared ideas. And then they got stuck. As they contemplated their options, they were polite with each other, no one wanting to hurt anyone's feelings.

After several weeks of little action and the clock ticking, someone had enough. She took a stand and made a clear, authentic statement about the project she wanted them to do and why. Once she spoke, another stepped in, speaking her truth. And another. The group listened to each other's heartfelt expressions. As they reflected on their exchange, their decision was clear. Only one project had characteristics that met some need that each participant had expressed. Out of passionate individual expression, collective commitment surfaced, and a clear purpose was named.

Later, I spoke with the woman who had jumped in first to learn what had prompted her action. She told me that it had been an important moment of letting go. She decided that making a meaningful choice was more important to her than maintaining her image. So she took a risk. That risk opened the way to authentic explorations of needs and longings. It surfaced differences among the women that helped them to coalesce around what really mattered. That moment of naming not only moved them to action, but also brought them closer together as a team.

═══════════

As this story shows, naming is both an end and a beginning. The women's search for a project came to a close with their newly discovered clarity. That clarity energized them for the next step of their journey: doing the service project. It also equipped them with deeper, more authentic relationships for the work ahead.

When something novel is named, we are transformed in some way. We may have more faith in ourselves or more compassion for others. We are likely to be more resilient, more tolerant of the unknown. We become a living part of a larger whole, which is a feeling difficult to forget and almost impossible to describe. Having experienced the magic, we may seek it again. If this sounds a bit mystical, try it. With repetition, it may become familiar, something that we have faith will happen routinely. Yet even as our confidence grows, we are unlikely to take it for granted.

TIPS FOR NAMING

Emergence culminates in naming. It is the moment when novelty arises.

CALL "IT" FORTH. Ask what wants to emerge. Then let go. It may not come. Yet I am amazed how often someone speaks unexpected wisdom that has everyone nodding yes.

SENSE THAT RING OF TRUTH. Listen for that moment of surprise and elation, when the diverse people of a system say yes to what arises. Amplify it. Celebrate it when it happens.

IF YOU FEEL AS IF YOU'RE WORKING TOO HARD, TAKE A BREAK. Naming can't be forced. If you keep working it, sometimes names become more elusive. If there's time, sleep on it. Social psychology offers a body of evidence showing that a night's sleep supports our ability to sort through complexity. In what is called the Zeigarnik effect, we continue processing uncompleted or interrupted tasks.[2]

Our unconscious helps new patterns to form that are too tough for our analytic mind. We have all experienced the effect of "sleeping on something" and having it come into greater clarity in the morning.

HAVE FAITH. Names arise in their own time. Though analysis may contribute information to the mix, ultimately, naming novelty into being is a complex, nonlinear act. Names arise spontaneously when conditions are ripe.

The magic of naming creates a challenge. How do we share the experience? What can move those who weren't present for the birth?

Harvest: Share Stories

Once meaning is named, how does it spread?

Stories help us to transition. They support us in making sense of what is ending and what is beginning. The arts—music, dance, poetry, film, painting, sculpture, theater, and so on—are powerful carriers of story. They assist in spreading meaning. For example, with rare exceptions, every social movement has songs. During the civil rights movement, the song "We Shall Overcome" instilled commitment to keep going even in the darkest times. Names like *industrial revolution, information age, women's movement,* each speak volumes about these accumulated moments in time. They are a shorthand that tells a story.

How we tell stories matters. Is the glass half empty or half full? Is the dying of newspapers a disaster for democracy or an opportunity for some new and better possibility? Since great stories have dynamic tension, it is likely both.

Harvesting stories helps us to share meaning. It carries the seeds of emergence beyond those who were part of a pivotal experience. Given the magnitude of the challenges we face, how can we possibly share meaning on a scale and at a speed that can make a difference?

My colleague Christine Whitney Sanchez faced this question on a national scale, working with Girl Scouts of the USA. Using a variety of harvesting modes, a transforming story of Girl Scouting was revealed, touching three million girls and one million adult volunteers.

From the beginning, the design team for the 2008 Girl Scout National Convention wanted girls to lead the way. Our vision was bold: Design a process that invited members to use their voices, have conversations that mattered, and self-organize to create the future of the Girl Scout Movement. Ten thousand Girl Scouts from around the world participated in the process.

As a lifelong Girl Scout, I was thrilled to head up a consulting team for the StoryWeaving Initiative. Powered by the passions of hundreds of volunteers, collective wisdom and a larger story of Girl Scouting emerged over the four days of the convention.

The team wove together conversation, story, and the arts using Appreciative Inquiry, Digital StoryWeaving, StoryLooms, Open Space Technology, and World Café to create a multimodal experience. While the specific methods weren't central, their spirit, principles, and practices made all the difference. They provided heart, creativity, and order to deal with the inevitable chaos resulting from this kind of process.

On opening night, members used appreciative questions, printed on "Keepsake Cards," to converse with new and old friends: "What brought you to this moment?" "Who has helped you to become a leader in this movement?" "What leadership lesson do you have to share?" A "texting poll"—messages entered by phone texting—captured the themes that the members heard in each other's stories. Real-time results scrolled onto the JumboTrons—big screens in the convention hall.

Fourteen- to 18-year-old girls, armed with Flip video cameras, became Digital StoryWeavers. They captured and produced leadership stories throughout the convention. The production room was abuzz from dawn to dusk, as digital interviews were woven into stories that later premiered on the JumboTrons. Digital StoryWeaving girls authored the larger story of "girl power" and distributed leadership emerging in the Girl Scout movement.

For those who were more tactile, StoryLooms were set up throughout the convention center. Members wove personal stories into the larger story. Girl Scouts of all ages brought fibers, yarns, strips of old camp T-shirts, weeds, leaves, bark, feathers, and almost anything else from nature to place within the fabric of the StoryLoom. While sharing their leadership stories, they created gifts of friendship and, as a result, a common call to action for the community of Girl Scouting.

Digital StoryWeavers captured the action during the Open Space on successful council membership practices. Self-organized conversations helped members to identify ways to bring the newly revitalized program to even more girls and to promote and expand the reach of Girl Scouting. The 242-page Book of Proceedings is available online.[3]

A Leadership Café, using the World Café process, surfaced ideas and wishes regarding Girl Scout leadership. A film crew captured the energy of this spontaneous conversation among hundreds of convention-goers. Two short videos on the essence of the World Café process are now available online.[4]

On the final morning of the convention, participants met in their geographic councils to discuss top priorities for the Girl Scout Movement and to identify their own commitments. Results were texted and bounced onto

Word Cloud of Commitments[5]

the big screens. Within 24 hours, a member of the StoryWeaving team had posted a word cloud—a visual depiction of the frequency of use of words— on the StoryWeaving site.

Bushels of collective wisdom were harvested at the convention.[6] With support from national staff and local volunteers, Girl Scout troops and local councils have brought the spirit of creative conversation home. They are living an emergent story of a Girl Scout Movement alive with girls in the lead that ripples to this day.

―――――――――――――

As the Girl Scout story shows, a great harvest takes many forms. With a mix of tools, technologies, artists, and formats, not only did convention-goers benefit from the harvest, but they continue to spread the story long after the end of the event.

TIPS FOR HARVESTING

Harvesting tells the stories that are ripe, seeding new possibilities in the process.

INVITE ARTISTS—BOTH DECLARED AND THE ONES WITHIN EACH OF US. Art—music, poetry, movement, visual arts—carries meaning. When artists are present or the artists within are invited to participate, they naturally harvest stories.

MAKE TOOLS AVAILABLE. Anticipate the need. Have supplies on hand: paper, markers, recorders, cameras—whatever can serve the harvest.

USE MANY MODES. Different people absorb meaning through different means. For many of us, the most effective stories are multimodal. Use text, images, movies, audio, and more.

SHARE THE ESSENTIAL STORIES. What meaning do we wish to share? What happened? How did it happen? Why does it matter?

THINK ABOUT WHOM WE WISH TO REACH AND HOW BEST TO DO SO. A combination of advance thought and ideas that surface in the moment clarify who can benefit from the stories and the forms that work to tell them.

Harvesting makes meaning of what happened and inspires us to engage in what's to come. It provides energy for doing it again . . . and again.

SEVEN

ITERATE: DO IT AGAIN ... AND AGAIN

*History doesn't repeat itself, but it
rhymes.*

—Mark Twain

Something subtle often happens after an experience with emergence. Whether it was living through an earthquake or hurricane or coming together with a diverse group to address an intractable challenge, life returns to normal. But not quite. Old habits seem strange. Normal activities seem more like walking through a dream. There is a Zen proverb: "Before enlightenment, chop wood, carry water. After enlightenment, chop wood, carry water." Though we may look the same, the experience changes us.

What keeps us going?

While emergence is how nature takes great, discontinuous leaps to create novel forms, it leaves many ripples in its wake. This chapter describes how those ripples are integrated into our assumptions about how our world works over time. It puts emergence into the bigger picture of change by discussing iteration—doing something again and again, each time influenced by the previous experience. It sheds light on an important and elusive challenge of change: sustaining the gains. By the end of this chapter, you should have a sense of how to work with the aftermath of emergence.

Integrating What's Novel into What We Know and What We Know into What's Novel

Not only are we changed when we experience emergence, but so are our relationships, how we interact with each other, and how we relate to our environment. Business as usual has been interrupted, compelling us to revise our understanding of who we are and what assumptions—the "simple rules" or invisible assumptions that guide our actions—we wish to embrace. We generally become more resilient, with increased capacity to work with differences and the unpredictable. We can sense in ways that weren't previously part of our makeup. Individually and collectively, we become more complex systems. It takes time to assimilate the new story of who we are; who "the other" is; how we fit together; what it means for ourselves, our relationships, our society; and how it shapes our actions. I had a personal taste of this shift following a trip to Russia. It taught me that making sense of an experience takes time.

━━━━━━━━━━

In 2000, I spent a month in Siberia. The group I traveled with had been advised to bring toilet paper from home. It was a good idea, because public restrooms had none. Midway through our trip, we hosted a weeklong leadership workshop for women who were starting social service organizations. They were replacing the social system infrastructure that had collapsed during perestroika. The U.S. team shared a space at the conference facility. We kept running out of the half-used rolls of toilet paper we were supplied each time we requested more. Three days in, I went to our room during a break to discover four unwrapped rolls. I was elated! I thought, "Maybe I should take some with me in case my supply from home isn't enough for the rest of the trip." And then it hit me: I knew the reason why public places had no toilet paper. If everyone followed my impulse and took a little home, public institutions would become everyone's TP suppliers! In the U.S., we have a story of abundant toilet paper. In Russia, there was a story of scarcity. I shared my insight with workshop participants. One of our translators told us that during her first trip to the U.S., she thought she was in toilet paper heaven. Toilet paper and our beliefs about scarcity and abundance became cultural metaphors for understanding the invisible assumptions that shape our lives.

As our travels continued, I noticed that the napkins in most places were small and one ply thick. Other cultural differences also caught my eye: converting dollars to rubles illegally on the streets was normal. Periodic and unpredictable power outages were frequent. Indoor plumbing was nonexistent outside the cities. Apartment buildings had no common areas. I remember my judgment about a government that had spent more money on the nuclear arms race than on basic infrastructure for its citizens. And my conclusion that when a government doesn't want people to organize, it designs buildings without a place for them to gather in community. Were these accurate interpretations of my observations? I don't know. I do remember on the plane home going into the restroom and being overwhelmed by the variety and abundance of papers: toilet seat covers, tissues, toilet paper, paper towels.

==

As is the case after encountering emergence, I was changed by my experience. My habitual patterns had been interrupted. With reentry to the United States, I was more aware of my surroundings. I understood that many assumptions I took for granted had different meanings to my Russian colleagues. I assimilated a new guiding principle: things are not always what they seem; do not assume I know what's going on based solely on my observations. Since the trip, I am less likely to jump to conclusions without checking with others on their perceptions. My toilet paper epiphany caused me to revisit some mundane assumptions. I hadn't noticed the abundance in my ingrained routine until it was absent. I am both more appreciative of the abundance in my life and more mindful of choosing less wasteful alternatives.

My trip to Russia is an example of weak emergence. I was different, perhaps more capable, but still able to assimilate these new aspects into my basic cultural narrative.

With strong emergence, everything we know is reordered around new organizing principles—the simple rules or assumptions we use to bring order to our lives. I have a colleague, Sabine Pannwitz, who grew up in East Germany when it was behind the Iron Curtain. We were walking along Unter den Linden (Berlin's equivalent to Paris's Champs-Élysées) to the Brandenburg Gate. She told me that this used to be the end of her world. It was where the Berlin Wall divided the city. She went on to tell me that she was in college when she emigrated to West Germany. It was tremendously disorienting. She came from a society that, once she had chosen her college major, selected every other aspect of her education. Her new West German university gave her complete freedom to choose her course of study. She told me she was so overwhelmed that she couldn't act. She had no preparation for making such decisions. Nor did she know how to face all of the little choices that are normal for westerners. How do you choose among dozens of brands of toothpaste? What differentiates one type from another? It took her years to learn how to function in her new home. She revisited virtually everything she knew about how things work, slowly integrating assumptions new to her that emerged as she learned how to fit into her new environment.

If one person freezes when faced with such change, imagine the effect when whole societies make such a shift, as East and West Germany did when they reunited. I had the privilege of witnessing a conversation among people from East and West Germany during a Future Search workshop in Berlin. I came to understand that although West Germany "won" with the dominant economic system, everyone lost. The countries came together without the sort of creative engagement through which East Germany's close-knit family and community relationships might have been valued as a gift to the re-knit society. East Germans integrated new operating principles, and West Germans provided the context. Perhaps a container, like Future Search, that allowed East Germans and West Germans to explore the best of both cultures might have led to a novel outcome with the economic vibrancy of the West and the community vitality of the East.

These stories highlight that it takes time to assimilate what emerges. Perhaps that explains why it often seems that after a powerful collective experience, nothing else happens for a long time.

Doing It Again ... and Again

Repetition and iteration are two forms of doing something over and over. In repetition, the same act continually recurs. I have heard insanity defined as doing the same thing repeatedly expecting different results. This type of static stability is useful for making widgets that have to fit with little tolerance for variation. In human systems, while the predictability may be nice, over time such rigidity can contribute to collapse. Just think of the images conjured by the organizational phrase "But we've always done it that way."

Iteration, by contrast, is a repeating process in which the output of the current cycle becomes input to the next cycle. With each execution, conditions evolve and affect the next cycle. Iteration describes how we learn.

Although this process looks straightforward on paper, in practice, several challenges arise when we attempt to understand how change occurs over time. The next few pages describe three challenges. First, changes may be virtually invisible in the beginning, accelerating with continued iterations. Second, emergent change arises in an almost untraceable flow, not the easy-to-follow cause and effect we can track through "managed change." Finally, change seems to have a spiral character, with aspects long discarded reemerging in a later iteration.

From Invisible Beginnings

The first time we pursue an intention, we might do it alone; but if we keep at it, it can gain traction. The initial inquiry may not attract anyone. For example, from quiet beginnings, a movement of storytellers introducing a sacred version of the story of evolution is growing. That growth highlights how we experience iteration in our social systems.

My colleague Michael Dowd is an evolutionary evangelist. Ever hear of such a role? If not, you may soon. Michael wrote a book, *Thank God for Evolution*, about the relationship between science and spirit.[1] To trace the path of his work, one could begin with a unique voice, Pierre Teilhard de Chardin. Teilhard de Chardin was a French philosopher and Jesuit priest whose book *The Phenomenon of Man* (1955) was an influential account of the cosmos unfolding. Many have read Teilhard de Chardin. No one could have predicted that one of those readers, theologian Thomas Berry, would dedicate his life to furthering these ideas. Nor that Berry would attract a young cosmologist, Brian Swimme, to coauthor a brilliant, poetic book, *The Universe Story*, that marries science and spirit.[2] Nor that others would read Teilhard de Chardin or Berry and Swimme, and, seeking more inspiration, would find each other. With each iteration, the merit of the ideas is affirmed and amplified. The number and variety of companions and sense of companionship also grow along the way.

The pace of growth among those now working at the crossroads of science and spirituality is accelerating. In addition to Michael Dowd, dozens of scientists, spiritual leaders, and social activists make the telling of a sacred evolutionary story part of their life's work. As they share their views, the ideas get clearer. Novelists, artists, poets, and musicians are inspired to tell the story through different modes of expression. As the story goes multimodal, it takes off. These ideas are everywhere—in songs, in novels, and on the news.

We are reintegrating views split when Western culture organized science and religion as incompatible ways of understanding our place in the universe. We have learned so much about cosmological, geological, and biological evolution. A richer, more complex sense, both scientific and spiritual, of how we fit in the cosmos is coalescing. Perhaps the universe story as a collective creation story is emerging now because we need it. It not only helps us to understand our place in the universe, but also makes it clear that we are part of a common family.

―――――――

From one voice to many, starting almost undetectably small, changing slowly and incrementally, then taking off. Since the 1950s, we've moved from an occasional voice to a few pioneers to many people making sense of the sacred and scientific story of our evolving universe. Because of his accessible style, Michael Dowd may be the one who breaks through to popular culture, putting to rest the war of words between science and religion that has gripped so many in the United States.

This pattern of change over time is visible in the power curve:

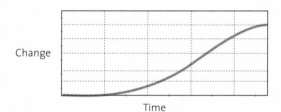

Most of us notice a shift only after it is well under way. Knowing this pattern may help some of us to keep going through the early, invisible times as we pursue our own initiatives. When we have just the whisper of an idea, getting started is an act of faith. If we don't see results from our efforts, most of us tend to move on, looking elsewhere to make a difference. Appreciating our effect is difficult when we can't see it. Most of us do better joining existing initiatives and organizations. For those called to initiate: consider staying with it even when faced with little or no visible results. The breakthrough may be just around the corner.

Ironically, radical shifts sometimes seem trivial at first. Integrating novelty takes time. We must bump into old assumptions and behaviors and notice that they no longer work. Then we try the new assumption or behavior instead. How long did it take e-mail to replace snail mail as our primary means of correspondence? The red ink in the post office and rising stamp prices are effects that have been in the making for years. How long will it take us to collectively sort out what communication technology to use when? I often leave voicemail, e-mail, and a text message when trying to reach someone in a hurry! Of course, these communication tools are the tip of one iceberg of that mammoth emergent agent of change called the Internet.

The fruits of emergence often ripen slowly. By the time most of us notice, it is a whirlwind that we can barely grasp. One need only listen to scientists continually revising their estimates of the speed of melting Arctic ice to understand that the pace is not linear.

When consciously working with change, remember that going to scale begins with a single step and then another and another. As energies ripen, the pace accelerates. Starting small, we learn the skills and presence to work with the unexpected. As capacity grows, we can take on more complex systems with more diverse participation and reach greater numbers. Journalism That Matters has been doing its work since 2001, including a three-year gap between the first three iterations before it took off. Now demand is accelerating. And we're better equipped to handle it.

Walking Randomly toward Coherence

Change rarely has a predictable progression. A random walk describes it better, with sparks appearing at unexpected moments. First small clusters form, then larger ones, coming together through interactions that seem to magically lead to increasing connections. Such is how networks grow. The leap in personal communications from letters to e-mail tells the tale. Correspondence used to be personal, a letter penned from one person to another. Carbon copy paper made business communications a bit more convenient. But personal letters remained just between friends. When e-mail arrived, it was simpler and faster to drop a quick line to a friend. Or two friends. Or 20. The one-to-one barrier was broken, and we could keep our friends tuned in as long as they, too, had an e-mail address. Pretty soon grandparents were logging in to connect with the grandkids. And acquaintances across oceans became friends without ever meeting face-to-face. One unintended consequence: the holdouts who opted not to go online find themselves increasingly outside the stream. They are isolated on the dry banks of an almost defunct and quaint form of communication now commonly called "snail mail." Another unintended consequence: personal communication has a radically different meaning as it goes online. It is perhaps both less personal and less communicative. Facebook, Twitter, and other social networking tools have enabled us to connect not just to our friends, but to our friends' friends. With the addition of likes, groups, and other ways of clustering, we are meeting up, linking in, and becoming increasingly connected with each other. Our connections may have greater reach and less intimacy. The many consequences won't be visible for a while. In the meantime, we are weaving a web of relatedness that circles the globe at an accelerating pace.

Change as a Spiral

Another notable aspect of change is characterized by the phrase "The more things change, the more they stay the same." Change spirals over time. It cycles through interactions that differentiate and coalesce, guided consciously or unconsciously by an intention. For example, the core intention of health care is to ensure our well-being. This purpose led to practices for doing whatever it took to keep people alive. Technologies changed. Now we can keep the body breathing even if the mind is gone. Social, emotional, economic, and other ripples from this shift affect individuals and society. The Terri Schiavo case pitted government and spouse against parents over whether to pull the plug on this young woman in a persistent vegetative state. It spurred us to collectively reexamine what it means to ensure well-being. The hospice movement is growing in strength. Death-with-dignity acts have passed in several states, making physician-assisted suicide legal. Is it controversial? Without a doubt. Still, a new coherence around an enduring principle of what it means to ensure well-being is coming around again in a new form. This spiral dance of change is never ending. And yet, many of us desire to hold on to the gains as they unfold.

Sustainability

Perhaps the most frequently asked question when people have been part of an emergent change process is, "How do we sustain this?" Some are speaking to the outcomes, the tangible results or commitments that arose from their interactions. Others refer to the deep connections with people they didn't know before, frequently with people from different backgrounds than their own.

Often, the people involved in hosting are ready to shed their mantle of leadership. They put all their energies into creating the fertile conditions for a diverse group to interact and produce something meaningful. And they can celebrate some likely results:

- People are stretched, refreshed, and clearer about their next steps.
- New and often unlikely partnerships form.
- New and revitalized initiatives take off.

Many of these outcomes will continue without further support from the hosts. They are fueled by excitement and commitment.

Still, the desire to sustain the results runs strong in most of us. Many focus primarily on the tangible outcomes—the products invented, the projects launched. Others thrive on the creative, engaged community that forms and seek to keep it alive. Social science research has taught us something about what it takes:

- An image of a desirable future compels us to act.

- Like most mammals, we thrive on mutual support.

- We can keep these flames alive by inviting new hosts to step in, bringing fresh energy and ideas.

- We can invest in infrastructure for communication, periodically coming together face-to-face or using conference calls and other technologies to share what's happening.

- Online social technologies can support continued conversation.

- We can learn more skills for hosting conversations and for engaging emergence so that the experience of productive interactions among diverse people becomes less exceptional, more normal.

All of these activities are valuable next steps. They come with a caution. Often, our wish for sustainability is an implicit desire for static, predictable, unchanging dependability. Such qualities come at a high cost. They contain the seeds of the next upheaval.

Approach sustainability with resilience in mind. Think of sustainability as the capacity of a system to remain congruent with changing realities. It can recover from disturbances and retain its essential identity, meeting its needs with attention to the ability of future generations to meet their needs. In her posthumously published book, *Thinking in Systems: A Primer*, Donella Meadows, the pioneering environmental scientist and founder of the Sustainability Institute, beautifully describes the difference between static and dynamic stability:

> Static stability is something you can see. It's measured by variation in the condition of a system week by week or year by year. Resilience is something that may be very hard to see, unless you exceed its limits, overwhelm and damage the balancing loops, and the system structure breaks down. Because resilience may

not be obvious without a whole-system view, people often sacrifice resilience for stability, or for productivity, or for some other more immediately recognizable system property.

I think of resilience as a plateau upon which the system can play, performing its normal functions in safety. A resilient system has a big plateau, a lot of space over which it can wander, with gentle, elastic walls that will bounce it back, if it comes near a dangerous edge. As a system loses its resilience, its plateau shrinks, and its protective walls become lower and more rigid, until the system is operating on a knife-edge, likely to fall off in one direction or another whenever it makes a move. Loss of resilience can come as a surprise, because the system usually is paying much more attention to its play than to its playing space. One day it does something it has done a hundred times before and crashes.[3]

Human systems are resilient when we cultivate both clear intentions and good relationships. If the focus is principally on projects, efforts die when the projects end. If, in addition to tending to projects, a shared intention and the social fabric are nurtured, a vibrant community of practice continues to generate creative responses to complex issues for a long time.

Leadership for engaging emergence involves stewarding shared intention and tending to the social fabric—both of which require welcoming spaces for conversation. Conversational leadership, like knowing how to engage emergence, invites us all into leadership work. This, too, is a turning of the spiral, redefining the who and what of leadership. We are in the midst of grappling with a new story that shifts leadership from tops of hierarchies to hubs of networks, a topic deserving of its own book.

TIPS FOR ITERATING

Emergence is part of a cycle of change. Doing "it" again ... and again reaps rewards over time.

STEWARD SHARED INTENTIONS. As events unfold, periodically affirm that our reason for being is still relevant and still fuels us. Revisiting intentions often reinvigorates and refreshes us, reminding us of why we said yes when the work gets hard.

TEND THE SOCIAL FABRIC. When people feel they belong, they show up, bringing their gifts. Coupled with shared purpose, a sense of community keeps the fires of commitment burning, fueling ever more creativity and innovation.

AS "IT" TAKES SHAPE, GIVE "IT" AWAY. The more attractive and accessible our outcomes, the more they inspire others to join in. New participants bring fresh energy and questions. Although disturbances are part of the package, we now know that just sparks creativity. Make it easy for people to get involved.

KEEP THE FAITH. The effects of our actions need time to take root and grow. If it matters, stay with it.

We have explored the nature of emergence and practices for preparing ourselves, for hosting, for engaging by stepping up and into emergence, and for keeping it all going. In part 3, we'll look at some principles that put these practices in context. The principles increase our understanding of the forces at play, freeing us to work more creatively with the practices.

PART III

Principles for Engaging Emergence

The bad news: there is no key to the universe.
The good news: it was never locked.

—Swami Beyondananda, *Ten Guidelines to Enlightenment*

A principle is a fundamental understanding or assumption that guides further understanding or action. Principles help us to make order out of chaos.

If practices guide us in *how* to do something, principles help us to sort through *what* to do. They describe the landscape, enabling us to discern useful characteristics so that we can make useful choices. Principles support us in designing our initiatives, organizing our work and ourselves, and determining what to do and how best to do it. For example, a commonly cited medical principle is "First, do no harm." This fundamental understanding informs life-and-death decisions without prescribing a specific approach.

I derived these principles for engaging emergence by connecting my understanding of emergent change processes with what science tells us about the dynamics of emergence. I asked:

If emergence occurs through

- simple rules,

- no one in charge,

- feedback between and among neighbors, and

- clustering of like with like,

what are the implications for how we engage with it?

The following five principles are my answer to this question. They support us in engaging emergence.

WELCOME DISTURBANCE. Disruption indicates that the normal behavior of a system has been interrupted. If we ignore the disturbance, chances are that conditions will get worse. If we get curious about it, the disruption could lead to breakthroughs.

PIONEER! Break some habits by doing something different. Prepare and jump into the mystery, working with the feedback that comes.

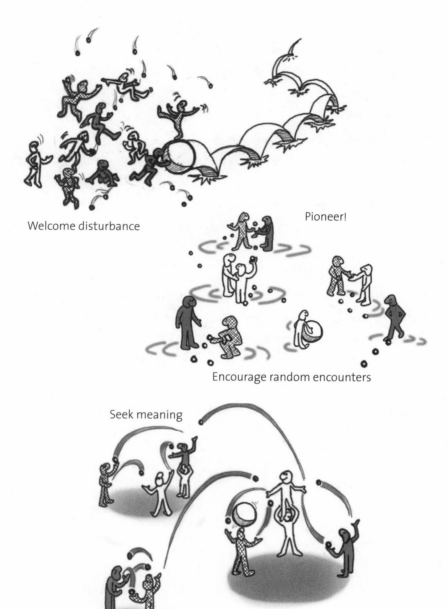

Welcome disturbance

Pioneer!

Encourage random encounters

Seek meaning

Simplify

Principles for Engaging Emergence[1]

ENCOURAGE RANDOM ENCOUNTERS. Remember, no one is in charge. More accurately, we never know which interactions will catalyze innovation. Maximize interactions among diverse agents, knowing that unexpected encounters will likely trigger a shift.

SEEK MEANING. Meaning energizes us. It orients us as coherence differentiates and renews itself. As we discover mutuality in what is personally meaningful, we come together. Like clusters with like. Shared meaning draws us to common awareness and action. When shared meaning is central, we organize resilient, synergistic networks that serve our individual and collective needs.

SIMPLIFY. Principles—simple rules—equip us to work with complexity. When principles break down and the situation grows chaotic, what is essential? What serves now? As answers coalesce, we become a more diverse, complex system around reformed principles at the heart of the matter.

The next five chapters delve more deeply into these principles. Each chapter contains a discussion, a story, and some practices that commonly support the principle.

EIGHT

WELCOME DISTURBANCE

Hopefulness only makes sense when it
doesn't make sense to be hopeful.

—Paul Hawken, commencement address, 2009

What is it like when our world is disrupted? How did autoworkers feel, not just losing their jobs, but losing a way of life that shaped their lives, their children's lives, their community's lives? We can easily say, "Serves them right for making an inferior product," in the abstract. I dare any of us to say it to a grieving member of the industry, someone who sees his or her work contributing to society.

Welcoming disturbance can move us from the pain of change to its possibilities.

How do we find potential in the midst of disruption?

Isn't it useful to know that order can arise out of chaos? Conflicts, differences, and disruptions are great indicators that we'd better act. Engaging emergence is a good strategy for taking on wicked problems. Knowing that we have a viable approach is a reason for optimism, not to mention untying a knot or two in one's gut. Rather than throwing our hands up, not knowing what to do, we can take action. We know practices for engaging emergence that can lead to higher-order solutions that are radically novel, coherent, persistent, whole, and dynamic, and that positively influence individual behavior.

With practice, it becomes easier to see opportunity in disruption, and to choose possibility when facing chaos and dissonance. Attitude matters. Remember, focusing on possibilities is a choice. Isn't that useful to realize when facing challenges that stop us in our tracks? The angst that generally accompanies upheaval is life energy. And it is laden with potential.

Since disruption is a given when something is differentiating, we might as well learn how to handle it well. We can cultivate resilience—the capacity to be calm in the storm or at least bounce back when hit. Most people take their cues from those around them. When we show up centered and calm, assuming that something useful can happen in the chaos, we bring others with us. The more we face the unknown with equanimity, seeking possibility, the more we send others the signal that they can too.

Practices that prepare us to engage emergence—*embracing mystery, choosing possibility*, and *following life energy*—help us to get started. In 2004, I was privileged to witness 30 Palestinian teachers find possibility in disruption when I led an Appreciative Inquiry (AI) workshop in Ramallah. The Appreciative Inquiry process is based in asking possibility-oriented questions that focus on what is working and what is possible, to inspire collaborative and wise action. (See "About Emergent Change Processes" for a description of the Appreciative Inquiry process.)

As the following story illustrates, welcoming disturbance helps us to find positive possibilities, courage, and companionship that enable us to act even in challenging situations.

As I prepared for the workshop, I asked my host for a theme we could use so that participants could experience Appreciative Inquiry. She told me that all Palestinians struggle with living with the occupation. I gulped when I got her message. How could I write appreciative questions about living with the occupation? It was beyond my experience. We settled on leadership as the theme. This first exchange was a hint that things might not go as expected as I headed into the mystery of an unfamiliar culture. I went with my ears and eyes wide open, receptive to what came my way.

By the end of day one, the group had identified characteristics of great leaders through an Appreciative Inquiry. I was troubled because they talked of leadership in the abstract, describing qualities they wanted in their president. Usually such an AI process would lead to insights into our personal power as leaders.

As day two dawned, I wanted to bring more of a spirit of possibility into the room. I was not sure how to do so. I just knew that was my intent. We began, sitting in a circle. I asked the group to reflect on the previous day. In a few minutes, someone began talking about how difficult her life was. Now "difficult" has a different meaning for someone who spends hours waiting to get through a checkpoint, or is separated from family by a wall, or who has seen property destroyed or loved ones hurt. Others started to complain. These folks lived with disturbance all the time! I took a deep breath, aware that their complaints were an opening. I asked if they would be willing to apply what they were learning about Appreciative Inquiry to their lives. They said yes. And I breathed a sigh of relief. They chose possibility.

They split into four groups and picked a topic on which to develop two appreciative questions: a personal story question and a future question. It was wild! They worked in Arabic, I'd check in, and they'd switch to English. Each group struggled to shift topics like "resisting the wall" and "fighting the checkpoints" to "working with the wall" and "useful checkpoints." Turning bitterness into productive questions was quite a reframing!

The group that chose "useful checkpoints" found a novel way to test their theme. They brainstormed a list of ways in which they had found checkpoints valuable. Mind you, this is a HUGE contradiction. I experienced a young Israeli soldier just doing his job, pointing a rifle at my head (from a distance) while his partner checked my papers. Many Palestinians face this experience every day. The list of benefits was amazing! It included: getting to know your neighbors, learning respect for elders (as they helped them to the front of the line), meeting new people. I knew something important was happening when the laughter became contagious.

As participants interviewed each other using their appreciative questions, I felt the energy in the room shift. When we debriefed, the responses were profound. With the occupation no longer a monolithic cause of anger and despair, the participants uncovered distinct aspects of it that gave them confidence and strength. Some of their insights: search for the good in everything; look at the problem from outside; determination leads to success; and meet the other as human. These folks, who had begun the day feeling powerless, found answers for retaining their dignity and power in an impossible situation. Life energy emerged from engaging their reality head on. They found ways to live creatively with the occupation, perhaps even for harvesting the seeds to end it.

———————

Had we not welcomed the angst into the room, participants would likely have left their authentic experiences outside. Had they left their authentic experiences outside, we would not have embraced the mystery of applying AI to a subject that mattered. Had we not applied AI to a subject that mattered, we would not have surfaced new possibilities. Had we not surfaced new possibilities, we would not have sparked the life energy that fueled new attitudes. Because we welcomed disturbance by embracing mystery, choosing possibility, and following life energy, we surfaced the means to meet upheaval with compassion, finding power over assumed destiny. What a lesson for the participants to take back to their students! They could equip their students to face disruptions with more compassion for themselves and for the Israelis with whom they are intertwined in a toxic situation.

PRACTICES FOR WELCOMING DISTURBANCE

Prepare

EMBRACE MYSTERY: SEEK THE GIFTS HIDDEN IN WHAT WE DON'T KNOW.

What does it take to be receptive to the unknown?

Let go of the need for immediate answers.

CHOOSE POSSIBILITY: CALL FORTH "WHAT COULD BE."

What do we want more of?

Seek positive guiding images.

FOLLOW LIFE ENERGY: TRUST DEEPER SOURCES OF DIRECTION.

What guides us when we don't know?

Work with the energies that are present.

Engage

INQUIRE APPRECIATIVELY: ASK BOLD QUESTIONS OF POSSIBILITY.

How do we inspire explorations that lead to positive action?

Ask questions that focus on a positive intention and invite others to engage with us.

While welcoming disturbance is largely about attitude, the next principle—pioneer!—provides guidance on what sort of action succeeds.

NINE

PIONEER!

Never tell people how to do things
. . . they will surprise you with their
ingenuity.

—General George S. Patton, Jr., *War As I Knew It*

Pioneers have much to teach us about engaging emergence. They begin their journeys into the unknown by marshalling resources and support. They are most resilient when they hold their intentions clearly but lightly, without attachment to specific outcomes. They adapt by welcoming feedback from others and the environment. Inviting partners with diverse perspectives and skills also increases their chances of success.

Pioneers know that the assumptions that work in familiar settings change when we enter the unknown. They know that breaking old habits takes courage. And while compassion may not be a traditional pioneering skill, it helps keep us going as we stumble through the many experiments that elate and frustrate along the way.

How do we discover our way forward?

Seek new directions. Think different.[1] Act courageously. If you are holding on, let go. If you are going with the flow, step out of the stream. If you are focused on the inside, see what's happening outside. If you are working downstream, check out what's going on upstream. Pioneering involves breaking habits, doing the unexpected, breaking well-worn feedback loops.

Although pioneering is a time to let habits go, they definitely have their use! Remember learning how to drive a car? It took tremendous energy and concentration. Once we learned the pattern—once it became a habit—we could focus our energy elsewhere. Reliability has value, so arbitrarily doing the unexpected is not desirable.

Still, when change is needed, habits can get in the way. Healthy change involves dynamic tension between our habits and our pioneering spirit. Without habit, function can't be sustained. But without disturbance, no learning or adaptation happens. We need the familiar and the strange, the comfort of repetition and habit, as well as the excitement and mystery of invention.

The art is in knowing when to embark on something new—and how—and when to stay with the flow. The environment is quite good at giving us feedback. We just need to listen and adapt to the signals we receive. When all is harmonious, proceed with business as usual. When dissonance appears, interrupt the habitual with something counterintuitive.

Here's a radical way of thinking differently about a signal: What if we viewed a terrorist attack as the system shouting at us? What message could such a vicious act contain that would be useful to our well-being? Such a question would take us into unexplored terrain. It could provide different feedback about the root causes of and responses to terrorism.

Asking habit-breaking questions uses all of our senses. Who and what we attend to matters. How diverse are the perspectives we hear?

People in the streets or on the front line have access to different information than those in elected office or in the boardroom. In how many ways are we tuning in? There's what we see, hear, taste, touch, and smell, as well as what we perceive through subtle senses, like intuition. Signals beyond a human scale are now visible via computers. Timing also matters. Delays in understanding climate change's signals challenge our ability to address its root causes. To do so requires massive changes of behavior. So how to begin?

Preparing as best we can before entering the unknown makes good sense. What are our strengths? What resources do we have? Whom should we invite to join us? Much like good hosting, equipping for an expedition into the unknown is well served by a clear intention, inviting diverse partners to join us, and welcoming what comes our way with a spirit of adventure. More, pioneers are masters of taking responsibility for what they love, following a calling that compels them to act.

Here's a story, told from my perspective, about embarking on a journey into the center of a controversy that involved some twists and turns. The story highlights what it takes to host an expedition when asking people to enter uncharted waters, and it illustrates a way to prepare for adapting to feedback in the moment.

————————

In 2005, a colleague, Sono Hashisaki, contacted me to work with her in a challenging situation. Four Pacific Northwest Indian coastal tribes were involved. So were the National Oceanic and Atmospheric Administration's Office of National Marine Sanctuaries (NOAA's ONMS) and the Olympic Coast National Marine Sanctuary (OCNMS) in Washington State. Over a two-year period, relations among the parties had become strained. They were further aggravated by a potential conflict. Unable to come to an agreement, the tribes took the situation to the Washington, D.C., office of NOAA's ONMS.

A meeting on "working out the issues and areas of conflict" was scheduled. The tribes chose Sono to facilitate because they trusted her. One challenge: no one thought anything useful would come of the meeting. A second challenge: before the session, the "feds" and the tribes were meeting separately to review their positions. What could Sono and I do that would make a difference?

As Sono painted the scene for me, we realized that the official reason for meeting and what the participants really wanted to accomplish weren't the same. We needed to create the conditions that would allow the organizations involved to address the conflict between them productively.

We chose to use Open Space Technology because it provides the lightest of touches. It poses a broad question and invites people to pursue what matters most to each of them. Since both sides were preparing for the worst, we set the stage with flexibility. Our intent was that the participants would work out their differences in real time.

On the morning of the meeting, formalities began with a tribal leader welcoming 18 people to the space. Sono and I launched the Open Space by inviting people to organize the agenda. Then we got out of the way. We sat on the sidelines as the first round of breakout sessions started. Sono briefed me on the relational dynamics at play—who sat with whom, who was left alone. One group focused on policy and governmental relations. Though chairs were close by, they stood, arms crossed, and talked for more than an hour. Finally, they relaxed, sat down, and moved into productive conversations right before lunch. Lunch proved to be a gestational (or digestive) time. When they reconvened, the four coastal tribes and the federal agencies came to an agreement in a record 20 minutes. The participants canceled their final round of breakout sessions, and we "circled up"—formed a circle—for a closing reflection.

During the closing, several people thanked their counterparts, saying it was one of the most respectful meetings they had ever had. A representative from the Bureau of Indian Affairs complimented all of them on the most productive meeting between federal officials and Native Americans he had ever witnessed.

We had done so little during the meeting yet got such great results! What had happened? We had done our homework, preparing for the unknown by using what we did know. From Sono's background work, we knew that expectations were low. We also knew the challenges we faced. With that in mind, we clarified the underlying intentions and shaped an organizing question accordingly. We used the simplicity of Open Space to create a spirit of welcome. The result of our work was conditions in which the group was able to adapt, no matter what arose. We confirmed that the people who attended could address the conflict. And we got out of the way, so that the meeting participants could take responsibility for what mattered to them.

PRACTICES FOR PIONEERING

FOCUS INTENTIONS: CLARIFY OUR CALLING.

What purpose moves us?

Tune in. Sense what is stirring in you, others, and your environment.

WELCOME: CULTIVATE HOSPITABLE SPACE.

How do we cultivate conditions for the best possible outcomes?

Create a spirit of welcome—physically, socially, intellectually, emotionally, and spiritually.

INVITE THE DIVERSITY OF THE SYSTEM.

How can we include the true complexity of the situation?

Reach out to those who ARE IN: with authority, resources, expertise, information, and need.

TAKE RESPONSIBILITY FOR WHAT YOU LOVE AS AN ACT OF SERVICE.

How can we use our differences and commonalities to make a difference?

Get involved with what matters, listening and connecting along the way.

LISTEN: SENSE BROADLY AND DEEPLY, WITNESSING WITH SELF-DISCIPLINE.

How do we more fully understand each other and our environment?

Pay attention using all of your senses to learn and adapt.

Pioneering develops flexibility, responsiveness, and resilience, schooling us in being sensitive to feedback. It helps us to experience the benefits of disruptions as possibilities surface. While it can be challenging, entering the unknown can also be exhilarating. And we never know which encounters will make the difference.

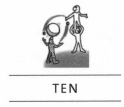

TEN

ENCOURAGE RANDOM ENCOUNTERS

*Life is the continual intervention of the
inexplicable.*

—Erwin Chargaff, *Heraclitean Fire*

Remember the notion that no one is in charge? This frequently cited characteristic of emergence reminds us that in complex systems, change doesn't happen through command and control. As appealing as it would be to tell a system what to do, where would you begin? Imagine commanding the health care system to be accessible and affordable. Even a CEO who gives an order that is inconsistent with expectations may have to wait a while to see it executed. Certainly in the economic crisis of 2009, auto executives learned the painful truth that they are not in charge of what happens! Changing systems, no matter the scale—families, work groups, organizations, economies, even our own behavior—is indirect. Although we can't tell a system to change, we can create conditions that support it in doing so.

What if we said, "Everyone is in charge"? Would that create better conditions for change? Consider the game of soccer. It is fluid, ebbing and flowing, highly interdependent and cooperative. Everyone matters.

The flow of the ball, the state of the field, the sounds of the crowd, all affect how the game unfolds. While "Everyone is in charge" might inspire more of us to engage, it still isn't quite on the mark. After all, the rules of the game and whom we will encounter are understood.

How do we create conditions in which chance interactions among diverse members of a system lead to breakthroughs?

This question is a conundrum at the heart of emergence that frustrates many and tickles some. We don't know which interactions or mix of interactions among us in what sequence catalyze emergent change.

Much of the magic of emergence arises from the unlikely encounters among us. An ancient rabbinic story states that since we can't recognize the Messiah in advance, it's a good idea to assume that it could be anyone. What a life-affirming stand! Anyone could be the one who names the unexpected insight or finds the synergy among us that makes the difference, a difference then magnified and evolved by the rest of us. Perhaps a time will come when that is predictable, but not today. Isn't it exciting that we can't tell what combination of knowledge, skills, and relationships could catalyze a breakthrough? Not if our only experience of conversation among people with conflicting perspectives is that it disintegrates into a shouting match. Then encouraging random encounters is likely to cause heartburn.

The good news is that emergent change processes have been successfully used to bring diverse groups of people who are in conflict together to accomplish useful outcomes for years. We know something about how to do the indirect work of creating conditions that will likely lead to emergence.

Further, trust, respect, and cooperation are not necessary preconditions, though they are frequent outcomes. In fact, conflict, distrust, and people locked in their positions are sources of life energy for engaging emergence.

Good hosting—with clear intentions and welcoming conditions— sets the stage for something useful to occur. Inviting people from all aspects of a system, complete with their conflicts, positions, and agendas, opens the way for creative engagement. Once people are present, inviting them to take responsibility for what they love as an act of service sparks them to fuel innovation that serves us all well.

Juanita Brown, creator of the World Café, shared a story with me about encouraging random encounters. The World Café process fosters strategic dialogue by creating a living network of connected small-group conversations focused on shared "questions that matter." The process encourages collective intelligence and committed action to emerge. (See "About Emergent Change Processes" for a description of the World Café process.)

The story describes what Samantha Tan, a former research fellow at Harvard University's Kennedy School of Government, uncovered in her native Singapore. It highlights the unexpected gifts that we receive from random encounters. In particular, it illustrates both the power and importance of discovering the common bonds among us.

The story begins when Samantha returned to Singapore to learn more about ways in which the World Café approach to large-scale dialogue and engagement was supporting Singapore's goal of becoming a "learning nation." The World Café process intentionally cross-pollinates diverse perspectives around critical questions in rotating rounds of conversation. It supports unexpected encounters and innovative possibilities for action.

Having worked as part of the government, Samantha sought to answer the question "How can we build bridges between those in power and other voices in our society so that something new can emerge?" Several vignettes of what she found on her Café learning journey provide a sense of what's been happening across Singapore.

Guns and Flowers

Senior and junior staff on the police force are sitting together in a Café conversation. People from three or four different ranks, wearing their uniforms and carrying their guns, are talking as equals at little Café tables with flower vases and checkered tablecloths. They are really listening and "hearing" each other's perspectives for the first time. For example, they discuss how street officers are affected by a computerized tracking system that's been installed in police cars.

After the Café, the senior officers say, "No matter how bright or smart our ideas are, we now realize that we need ideas from the people at the ground level to make policies that work." The junior officers come to appreciate that the seniors aren't just authoritarian. They really are concerned about the welfare of the junior members.

Nourishing Community Innovation through Dialogue

The People's Association of Singapore, through the National Community Leadership Institute (NACLI), decides to merge the World Café with our local culture. They create P2P (People to People) conversations between government representatives from different departments and grass-roots leaders of varied ethnic groups and perspectives. They use a creative adaptation of the World Café called the Knowledge Kopitiam. *Kopitiams* are traditional Singaporean neighborhood coffee shops that local people have gone to since our early immigrant days.

NACLI launches its Knowledge Kopitiams by re-creating a traditional kopitiam setting for its conversations. They call the kopitiam approach the "knowledge-traveling process." NACLI's magazine, *Kopi Talk*, spreads the word about this "old/new" way of encouraging innovative ideas among diverse constituents on key issues. The kopitiam idea begins to spread.

After experiencing the Knowledge Kopitiams and the creative ideas that emerge from them, Yaacob Ibrahim, then senior parliamentary secretary for the Ministry of Communications and Information Technology, comments, "Today we want to spark a revolution. Not to overthrow the government, but to reinvent ourselves. . . . These people-to-people discussions are essential to our development as a cohesive and well-informed people."

What Does It Mean to Care?

For me, the most surprising Café discoveries about the power of unexpected encounters came at the end of my visit. It was the last Café I participated in. Key organizational learning practitioners from the Police Department and the Housing Development Board convened the session. We put the question "What does it mean to care?" at the center of the Café. As Singaporeans, we often see ourselves primarily as logical, rational, efficient, and results oriented. We wanted to see what might unfold if we approached our national development from a different lens.

Something happened that afternoon that revealed our deeper common yearning for reaching across boundaries of class, ethnicity, gender, power, and other dimensions that so often separate us. There was a plainly dressed woman in the Café who seemed out of place, although I knew she'd been invited. I'd describe her as a "tea lady"—a service person who is usually pretty invisible in our society.

We were in the whole-group conversation at the end of the Café rounds. Having talked with many new people, the "tea lady" courageously stood up and said softly, but with much certainty, "You know, it's important to feel people care because when people care, it makes life worth living." The room was struck silent by her piercing humanity. Her words spoke to a national issue— our utilitarian mindset where people sometimes feel like widgets—and how debilitating and soul destroying it is. I was moved. Everyone was moved. And in that room, I knew that policy decisions would be shifted because of her unexpected contribution. That moment changed me forever.

Such simple words, with so much impact. Possibilities surface from unexpected encounters. As people randomly moved between café tables, their interactions generated increased understanding, sparked new ideas, and surfaced unspoken common yearnings. They found meaning that none could have uncovered on their own.

PRACTICES THAT ENCOURAGE RANDOM ENCOUNTERS

FOCUS INTENTIONS: CLARIFY OUR CALLING.

What purpose moves us?

Tune in. Sense what is stirring in you, others, and your environment.

WELCOME: CULTIVATE HOSPITABLE SPACE.

How do we cultivate conditions for the best possible outcomes?

Create a spirit of welcome—physically, socially, intellectually, emotionally, and spiritually.

INVITE THE DIVERSITY OF THE SYSTEM.

How can we include the true complexity of the situation?

Reach out to those who ARE IN: with authority, resources, expertise, information, and need.

OPEN: BE RECEPTIVE.

How do we make space for the whole story—good, bad, or indifferent?

Be willing to be more in questions than answers.

TAKE RESPONSIBILITY FOR WHAT YOU LOVE AS AN ACT OF SERVICE.

How can we use our differences and commonalities to make a difference?

Get involved with what matters, listening and connecting along the way.

CONNECT: BRIDGE DIFFERENCES AND BOND WITH OTHERS.

How do we link ourselves and our ideas with others similar to and different from ourselves?

Listen for deeper meaning, to seek common ground.

Acknowledging that we don't know which interactions matter sets up a different ethic for whom we include and how we interact. It encourages us to focus on teasing out the potential in the unknown. We can discover meaning, deep connections, and innovative ideas among us when we do.

ELEVEN

SEEK MEANING

There's a world of difference between
truth and facts. Facts can obscure the
truth.

—Maya Angelou, in *I Dream a World: Portraits of*
Black Women Who Changed America

For many, entering the unknown of emergence is akin to experiencing a dark night of the soul—an internal struggle, a questioning of one's purpose, that often leads to a spiritual awakening. Why do it without believing that it will lead to something useful . . . more than useful, something deeply meaningful?

Without meaning, nothing jells. Oren Lyons of the Iroquois nation states it eloquently: "We talk until there's nothing left but the obvious truth." Such truth is the threshold for action. When we can all find meaning in what emerges, something palpable shifts in our relationship with each other and ourselves. Our perception of the whole of which we are a part is more nuanced, more richly textured. Diverse perspectives no longer separate us. They connect us more deeply.

How do we surface what matters to individuals and to the whole?

Given time to reflect, we humans have a natural capacity for recognizing patterns, discovering coherence where none previously existed. But which patterns matter? How do we surface the ones with legs that move us?

When emergent change practitioners bring together diverse, conflicted groups around subjects they care about, it is like watching evolution through time-lapse photography. An attractive organizing intention provides an initial orientation. Yet people often enter angry or confused, full of distrust, holding firm to a position. Chances are, these feelings arise because many of them are understandably attached to what currently gives them meaning. Good hosting creates conditions that encourage authentic interactions. It supports them in loosening their grip on what they hold dear. In the process, meaning that connects a more complex and diverse mix of people and ideas can arise. Perhaps a conversation happens among a small, random cluster. Cued by implicit and explicit signals that different perspectives are welcome, the exchanges grow in civility. Participants become more curious about each other. As they open up, they may share what they love or what hurts, what makes them angry or what they fear. Once emptied of whatever baggage they brought, they speak of what they long for, their hopes and dreams.

At some point, there's laughter—a sign that the energy has shifted. It is like a phase transition from ice to water. Less energy is needed to tend the whole as people begin taking responsibility for their own behavior. They start caring for each other. Groups separate and re-form, the members carrying the seeds of their encounters. Many are touched by the experience. They continue mingling with others, and something remarkable begins to happen.

People connect with others around a few key ideas. They might even discover that they like each other, or at least respect each other.

They notice that the same themes are surfacing everywhere. Like attracts like. Before they know it, clusters form. Without any attempt to reach widespread agreement, a sense of commitment to a shared whole arises. People discover that what is most personally meaningful is also universal. While maintaining each person's distinctiveness, they become a social body connected through shared meaning.

A network grows in real time. No one orchestrates who connects with whom. Neighbors interact around whatever they find meaningful. Some feel so attracted to the cause that they become hubs in a network. They draw others to them, and clusters grow larger as the members bring their connections with them. Then one hub connects with another hub, and something coalesces, with hundreds, thousands, or even millions of people involved. Spirit is renewed; perhaps wisdom—knowledge and knowing deeper than the rational mind—is gained. Some deep truth is reignited. The form is novel, elegant, dynamic yet stable. It is more complex and more inclusive. Such is the potential of seeking meaning.

Consider the implications when technologies like Twitter support spontaneously organizing crowds with a cause. Retrospectively, Twitter may be cited as the reason why protests following Iran's June 2009 election were supported around the world. Activists on the ground in Tehran used Twitter to interact with each other and with the world outside. Rapid feedback affirmed an increasingly clear message: the future is in the hands of the people.[1] The sheer force of numbers coming together pressured a repressive regime from within and without. While the life-and-death struggle for the soul of that nation continues, the trajectory of events like the Iranian election is clear. As social network technologies enable increasingly complex order, governments that don't reflect the voice of the people will have a tough time maintaining control.

Technology plays an important role in finding shared meaning at scale. With its swift feedback and broad reach, the Internet is accelerating the pace and increasing the numbers of us who can participate. Something novel is emerging, enabled by technology. Something simple, yet quite complex. And deeply meaningful.

What supports such possibilities to emerge? Whether at the magnitude of a nation, an organization, or a small group, seeking shared meaning involves bringing forth authentic voices to air and explore differences. Circle Process provides a lens into what takes place at any scale. It elicits deep speaking and listening that seems to arise from the form itself—a ring of chairs and a clearly defined purpose. (See "About Emergent Change Processes" for a description of Circle Process.)

Christina Baldwin, PeerSpirit Circle Process consultant-author, puts it this way: "When people put chairs in a circle, it shifts the dynamic of a group. Leadership is embedded within the group and within the process. Shifting shape helps open the emergent conversation by focusing on the rim *and* the center."

In their several decades of refining PeerSpirit Circle Process, Christina and her partner, Ann Linnea, have become careful designers of social space capable of holding a group together while it explores issues of diversity, wholeness, and meaning. Says Ann, "In Circle Process, we design a tangible center that elicits the search for coherence in the group. We have been known to carry a bicycle wheel into an organization to demonstrate how the edge and the center of the circle are connected. We count on every person to speak their truth, and we count on each one to energetically address comments to the center so the hub is strong. The center represents a shared purpose, task, or question. The rim represents divergence."

Circle Process brought highly divergent opinions together in the national board of the Financial Planning Association (FPA), an organization formed out of two previously competing entities. Christina tells the story of how Circle Process supported FPA in using its diversity to find shared meaning.

Former board member and president Elizabeth Jetton described the situation to me when we began: "Two organizations glued themselves together with the shared belief that it was time to be one association. But we had no process for that emergence to occur. Our first meeting was with Robert's Rules of Order, a gavel, and chairs facing a panel of staff and directors. We brought the question 'Who are we going to be now?' But there was no way to talk about it in the format of the meeting. We spent a painful year, with lots of facilitators coming and going and a sense that to discover some kind of cohesiveness, we needed to get away and talk with and listen to each other."

The board had already shifted the chairs into a circle before Ann and I got involved. But they had not yet understood the notion of a center. Trust didn't exist. People had misused power as decisions were made (or unmade) in committees, in subgroups, or at the hotel bar late at night. Those decisions were not always shared with the whole board.

I coached a board meeting in October 2002, convened to refine the organization's sense of purpose and functionality. I found 40 board members and staff in a huge conference room sitting in a large circle with a bare hotel coffee table in the center. They used a hand-held microphone to pass the sanction to talk from person to person.

I watched them check in throughout the morning. Some people were brief, some long-winded. I could sense tension between members with differing ideas. Several spent their time in diatribes refuting previous speakers. The verbal energy was zinging around the space. Shared meaning was absent. At an appropriate coaching moment, I suggested the process would significantly improve if everyone spoke to the center, introducing the bicycle wheel imagery. Two young board members volunteered to design a meaningful focal point during the noon break.

When we came back in the room, the volunteers had carted in brick-sized stones from the hotel landscaping. They made a four-foot fire ring on the carpet using small branches pruned off the hotel shrubbery to construct a tipi "fire." Small orange gourds represented the flames. It was an unusual leap for a group of financial planners! Folks were amused, yet they took it seriously. The young planners explained that they hoped this fire circle would allow the group to get to the heat of their issues. They invited each person to offer their comments as fuel serving a common goal. They also placed four bowls of smooth stones around the circle, suggesting that whenever a person heard someone else make a comment that advanced shared meaning, they put a stone in the fire to acknowledge the contribution.

The board chair brought up the next topic and passed the microphone to garner commentary. Facing the "fire," they began to see their divergent voices feed the flame. Men who had been in heated opposition placed stones acknowledging their opponents. People stopped competing. When they needed to vote, board members rolled their conference chairs closer to the fire to see and hear each other without the mike. The staff held the outer rim. Building on this success, the next day they did the "paperwork"—breaking into small groups to craft agreements of self-governance, set goals, and articulate a vision statement that has kept them focused ever since.

Marv Tuttle, current executive director, often speaks about FPA's dedication to alternative group processes to other association leaders. "When I tell them we do three-day board meetings in circle with small groups operating in Open Space and that we do World Café with hundreds of members, they don't know what to think. Planners tend to be entrepreneurial, go-getters, quick thinkers. I explain that circle teaches us to hold long, sustained conversations that lead to a clear decision point. We have held substantial conversations about standards in the financial services industry. For example, it took us five years to come to a decision to press a lawsuit—which we won—with the Securities and Exchange Commission. We were clear about our intentions going into the suit, thanks to the long, clarifying, open-ended conversations we had in circle. Sometimes it makes the hair on the back of my neck stand up when we get to a point of understanding our commitment to an issue or each other. You don't get that in usual meetings."[2]

As the FPA story demonstrates, meaning emerges when we find our center. Shared meaning emerges when our individual centers connect to a commonly held center. Circles, with their hub and rim, make this notion of center visible. Networks are formed as many hubs connect, taking this pattern to scale. An important clue of new organizational forms resides in understanding that meaning connects us.

Whether in a network, hierarchy, or other shape, shared purpose binds us together. Finding the center happens when we give ourselves time and space to discover how the differences among us coalesce into a coherent whole.

PRACTICES FOR SEEKING MEANING

OPEN: BE RECEPTIVE.

How do we make space for the whole story—good, bad, or indifferent?

Be willing to be more in questions than answers.

LISTEN: SENSE BROADLY AND DEEPLY, WITNESSING WITH SELF-DISCIPLINE.

How do we more fully understand each other and our environment?

Pay attention using all of your senses to learn and adapt.

CONNECT: BRIDGE DIFFERENCES AND BOND WITH OTHERS.

How do we link ourselves and our ideas with others similar to and different from ourselves?

Listen for deeper meaning to seek common ground.

REFLECT: SENSE PATTERNS, BE A MIRROR.

What is arising now?

Get curious. Ask questions that tease out what is coming into being. Be a witness for another.

TAKE RESPONSIBILITY FOR WHAT YOU LOVE AS AN ACT OF SERVICE.

How can we use our differences and commonalities to make a
difference?

*Get involved with what matters, listening and connecting along
the way.*

Seeking meaning brings us together around what is most fundamental to us collectively, without asking us to sacrifice our individuality. Tradeoffs and compromises are not required in order for
individuals and the collective to discover shared meaning. Rather, we
allow simplicity to arise.

TWELVE

SIMPLIFY

The obvious is that which is never seen
until someone expresses it simply.

—Kahlil Gibran, *The Garden of the Prophet,*
    Lazarus and His Beloved, Sand and Foam

Order arises when individuals follow simple rules or organizing assumptions: Drive on the correct side of the road. Raise your hand and wait to be called on to speak. Rules provide structure and boundaries.

To a surprising extent, we don't have to articulate the rules. Initial conditions tell us a lot about the principles that guide us. Think how differently we feel when we walk into a softly lit room, music playing quietly in the background. Now think about entering a sterile meeting room with chairs all facing the front of the room. With no explanation, each situation sets up a different emotional response and tells us a lot about what is expected of us. Now that's simplicity!

What is the least we need to do to create the most benefit?

Given the complexity of human systems, how can we possibly know what sort of rules will create the desired changes to a system? Finding simplicity is an art of discovery, continually doing one less thing while seeking the heart of the matter. Getting to fundamentals is key. What is our purpose in seeking change? Who needs to be involved? How do we approach it?

Finding such answers is more art than science, and yet we do have some knowledge. We know, for example, that most of us take our cues from a mix of the environment—what others are doing—and our internal guidance system, shaped by our consciousness and our habits. While we can start anywhere, tuning in to our own motivations, aspirations, and dreams for the systems we are part of opens the way to an initial clarity. That clarity shapes our work.

The environment speaks volumes about who and what are welcome. It is rife with implicit rules that influence individual behavior. Despite such seeming complexity, the simple acts of focusing intentions and thoughtfully preparing welcoming conditions eliminate the need for countless explicit rules of behavior. While we don't want to oversimplify in ways that deny the real complexity we're dealing with, we do want to find simplicity that gets right to the heart of the matter. That simplicity taps fundamental truths underlying the complexity we face.

An inspiring example of what is possible when working from an ethic of simplicity occurred in a South Africa still under the shadow of apartheid. In 1991–1992, Adam Kahane worked with 22 prominent South Africans from across the ideological spectrum—politicians, activists, academics, and businesspeople—to develop and disseminate a set of stories about what might happen in their country over the next ten years. The "Mont Fleur project" started shortly after Nelson Mandela was released from prison. The African National Congress (ANC) and other organizations had been legalized, and the first all-race elections of 1994 had not yet been held.

The work involved reflection, naming, and harvesting. It explicitly did not directly link to action. For Western culture, which sets a high value on action, cultivating the capacity to reflect—to contemplate—is both challenging and essential. Since emergence cannot be forced, reflection aids us in participating with emergence as it arises. Reflection also supports us in uncovering the inherent simplicity of emergent complexity. Kahane's story holds many lessons for understanding simplicity.[1] Among them: Finding simplicity is not always simple. Uncovering it is indirect, taking patience, authenticity, and courage. Simplicity is linked to meaning. We can uncover it through reflection, and take it to scale by naming what is essential and by sharing the harvest of stories.

Dozens of "forums" were set up in South Africa, creating temporary structures that gathered together the broadest possible range of stakeholders to develop a new way forward in a particular area of concern. The Mont Fleur project was one type of forum that, uniquely, used the Scenario Thinking methodology—a process for generating stories of alternative plausible futures to arrive at a deeper understanding in order to improve current and future decisions. [See "About Emergent Change Processes" for a description of the Scenario Thinking process.]

The scenario team met three times in a series of three-day workshops. After considering many possible stories, the participants agreed on four scenarios that they believed to be plausible and relevant:

OSTRICH—A negotiated settlement to the crisis in South Africa is not achieved, and the country's government continues to be nonrepresentative.

LAME DUCK—A settlement is achieved, but the transition to a new dispensation is slow and indecisive.

ICARUS—Transition is rapid, but the new government unwisely pursues unsustainable, populist economic policies.

FLIGHT OF THE FLAMINGOS—The government's policies are sustainable and the country takes a path of inclusive growth and democracy.

The group developed each of these stories into a brief logical narrative. A 14-page report was distributed as an insert in a national newspaper, and a 30-minute video combined cartoons with presentations by team members. The team then presented and discussed the scenarios with more than 50 groups, including political parties, companies, academics, trade unions, and civic organizations. At the end of 1992, its goals achieved, the project was wrapped up and the team dissolved.

The ideas in the Mont Fleur team's four scenarios were not in themselves novel. What was remarkable about the project was the heterogeneous group of important figures delivering the messages, and how this group worked together to arrive at these messages.

Mont Fleur did not resolve the crisis in South Africa. The participants did not agree upon a concrete solution to the country's problems. The Mont Fleur process only discussed the domain that all of the participants had in common: the future of South Africa.

Among the four scenarios, only one story led to a sustainable outcome:

The simple message of Flight of the Flamingos was that the team believed in the potential for a positive outcome. In a country in the midst of turbulence and uncertainty, a credible and optimistic story makes a strong impact. One participant said recently that the main result of the project was that "[w]e mapped out in very broad terms the outline of a successful outcome, which is now being filled in. We captured the way forward of those committed to finding a way forward."

Similar efforts, with Kahane's support, are under way in Israel, Paraguay, Guatemala, Colombia, and Argentina.[2] May they bring similar success.

In part, what is striking about Mont Fleur is that the participants faced one of the most complex social challenges of modern times and catalyzed a shift through a simple process. A group embodying the whole system engaged in creative conversations about possible futures over nine days. Additionally, the members agreed to share the message broadly: four stories that "gave vivid, concise names to important phenomena that were not widely known, and previously could be neither discussed nor addressed."[3] The simplicity of both the process and its message contributed to a nation's returning to itself and the embrace of the international community.

Designing Conversations That Matter

The role of simplicity in design of conversational processes deserves exploration. Most of us don't think in terms of designing conversations. We just have them. Yet the emergent change processes that shaped this book are all about designing conversations that matter. The people who created the different processes took the everyday work of conversation and teased apart what makes the most difficult interactions succeed. They designed processes accordingly.

As the number of emergent change processes has grown, people like me have sought to understand what principles the different processes share. We wish to make it easier for anyone to know how to have the difficult conversations that matter.

Simplicity is design's holy grail: aesthetically pleasing, energy efficient, broadly effective. Principles and practices that help us know how to prepare, host, and engage support our sense of safety, comfort, creativity, curiosity, and authenticity. Harrison Owen, creator of Open Space Technology, introduced me to an elegant design question: What is one less thing to do and still be whole and complete? It is a disciplining question. Continually asked, it reveals the essence at the heart of what matters.

Oliver Wendell Holmes said, "I would not give a fig for the simplicity this side of complexity, but I would give my life for the simplicity on the other side of complexity." Are five principles for engaging emergence too few? Are they too many? Are they the principles that focus on the aspects of engaging emergence that matter most? Time will tell as we continue to experiment with the simple rules that create coherence out of chaos.

PRACTICES FOR SIMPLIFYING

REFLECT: SENSE PATTERNS, BE A MIRROR.

What is arising now?

Get curious. Ask questions that tease out what is coming into being. Be a witness for another.

NAME: MAKE MEANING.

How do we call forth what is ripening?

Be receptive to a leap that can come from anywhere.

HARVEST: SHARE STORIES.

Once meaning is named, how does it spread?

Tell the stories. Write, draw, sing, dance, etc. Capture the spirit in print, video, online, and other media. Since we absorb more through multiple forms of expression, the more media, the better.

ITERATE: DO IT AGAIN . . . AND AGAIN.

What keeps us going?

Integrate what we know into what's novel and what's novel into what we know.

We have explored both practices and principles for engaging emergence in parts 2 and 3. In the spirit of simplifying, 15 practices are expressed through five principles. While the principles capture a deeper essence of engaging emergence, they don't replace the practices. They serve different purposes. The principles help us understand what to do, and the practices help us understand how to do it. The more experienced we are, the easier it is to work from the simpler but more abstract form of the principles.

We have one last stage in our journey to understand this system for engaging emergence. Part 4 simplifies even further, posing three questions. They provide a philosophical context that offers a point of view for approaching emergence compassionately, creatively, and wisely.

PART IV

Three Questions for Engaging Emergence

*A good question is never answered. It is not a bolt to be
tightened into place but a seed to be planted and to bear more
seed toward the hope of greening the landscape of ideas.*

—John Ciardi, *Manner of Speaking*

The three questions below orient us to a fundamental pattern of change: *disturb*, *differentiate*, *cohere*. They help us to think strategically about how to work with change, particularly emergent change, by offering guidance on useful actions: *disrupt*, *engage*, and *renew*. The qualities that the questions suggest for those actions provide a philosophical context for achieving the best possible outcomes: *compassion*, *creativity*, and *wisdom*.

Like all appreciative questions, they direct our attention and open us to exploration. They are posed as questions rather than statements to remind us that when the terrain is uncertain, focus and fluidity both support us to be nimble in our response.

You can use them as you might an affirmation. Just as affirmations help us attend to what we wish to create, these questions help us adapt to the specifics of our situation. We can connect a pattern of change itself to our circumstances, by asking, "In this situation . . ."

- How do we disrupt coherence compassionately?
- How do we engage disruptions creatively?
- How do we renew coherence wisely?

These questions create temporary shelter in which we can consider the challenges of a changing system. They help us to experience and offer compassion in disruption, engage creatively with difference, and support both personal and collective renewal as potentially wise responses coalesce.

If you are familiar with Zen Buddhism, think of the questions as koans—paradoxical riddles or anecdotes that have no solution. If you seek to understand them in an intuitive way and work with them in your life, they may provide flashes of insight into what's going on and how to engage it.

The three chapters that follow each elaborate on a question.

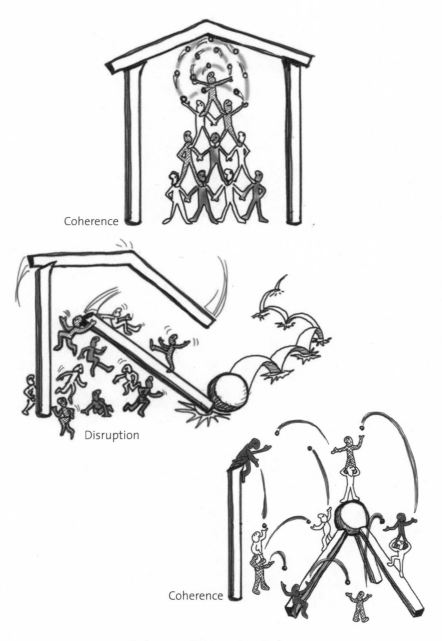

Coherence

Disruption

Coherence

Cohere—Disrupt—Cohere[1]

How do we disrupt established patterns, explore the diverse, often conflicting aspects of our system; and discern the differences that make a difference so that coherence arises anew and serves us well?

THIRTEEN

HOW DO WE DISRUPT COHERENCE COMPASSIONATELY?

*You've got to be careful if you don't
know where you're going because you
might not get there.*

—Yogi Berra, *What Time Is It? You Mean Now?*

B y now, it's clear: disruption, upheaval, conflict, and disturbance interrupt the current state. They reveal unexpected aspects of a system, differentiating some element or elements that were previously invisible. Perhaps the issue is civil rights: people of color or those with disabilities saying we have a place, too. Or maybe nature reminds us that we are not as independent from our environment as we thought. Disruptions help us to notice differences that are ignored aspects of our systems.

This chapter explores a role that disruption plays in emergence: surfacing useful distinctions. It introduces *compassion*—the capacity to enter into and be moved by another's experience—and it describes the relationship between compassion and disruption. It offers tips for cultivating compassion and a powerful practice of compassion—hearing, seeing, and loving. The chapter explores the question of when it makes sense to disrupt. It shares a story of learning how to compassionately disrupt in a situation in which one person seemed to be the disturbance. It ends with tips for disrupting coherence compassionately.

Using Disruption to Surface Differences That Make a Difference

Sometimes we shut down when facing disturbance; sometimes we open to possibilities. How we respond is a choice. The more open we are, the more likely we are to notice the creative potential. Consider these responses to the emotional roller-coaster of journalism:

- The *Seattle Post-Intelligencer* has closed its doors, part of the wave of newspapers folding. Who's next?
- I've taken a buyout and have done public relations work for a year. How can I find my way back into the journalistic work I find meaningful?
- With journalism in such upheaval, what do I tell my students?
- If not gatekeepers, what is our role?
- As a reporter, how do I interact with the audience?
- With ad revenues falling, what is the business model that can sustain journalism?
- How do I connect my community in civil conversation so that news engages more than just professionals?

Whatever your opinion of journalism, good information—and conversation—is essential to democracy. As people make sense of the shifting landscape, their perspectives surface different aspects to explore. Inherent in the responses above are the differences that make a difference: organizational resilience, the journalist's role, educating the next generation, revenue sources, meeting the investigative needs of communities, the relationship between journalist and audience. Journalists are revisiting all of these and other operating assumptions. What endures? What changes? Disruptions help tease out distinctions so that we can see them more clearly. They help us to see our system as a whole in all of its complexity by opening us to new facets of what we face.

Until the recent arrival of social media, journalism's form had been stable since the 19th century. No wonder those who grew up inside that system are disoriented, angry, fearful, or grieving as it falters. Yet it is hard not to be swept up in the enthusiasm of new media people who are inventing its future by turning old operating assumptions on their head. The interplay between those in mourning and those inventing creates a wild mixture of pleasure and pain. To borrow a phrase from Margaret Wheatley, we are hospicing the old and midwifing the new.

You might ask, "With so many disruptions coming at us, why disrupt anything? Why don't we just figure out how to respond?" In fact, where there's a natural or human-made disaster—a tornado, a financial crisis, something outside our control—most of us spend little time finding someone to blame. We just act. When we are out of immediate danger, we can contemplate prevention of or preparation for a recurrence.

Still, whether we like it or not, disruptions that affect us may cause us to disrupt others. Take, for example, a newspaper editor who is laying off 40 people because his paper is dying. He is in the midst of creating upheaval, however reluctantly, and wonders how to do that well.

Compassionate Disruption as an Entry to Engaging Emergence

Compassion helps us to face disruption, whether we cause it or are on its receiving end. Disrupting compassionately is an aikido strategy that grows our capacity to deal with difference, upheaval, conflict, and the unknown. Whether we are outside a system wanting in, inside the system wanting to change it, or even faced with an unexpected event, like a hurricane or an accident, bringing compassion into the equation shifts our focus and our options. It aids us when we create disruptions, providing a velvet glove for addressing a difficult situation.

Compassion, at root, means to suffer together. It honors our common humanity. Whether we cause or simply get caught in a disruption, compassion means that we face the situation together. In the most challenging situations, choosing compassion can bring us comfort, strength, and courage. Compassion helps us to speak our truth, even if we're angry or grieving, connecting us even as it differentiates what matters to each of us. With practice, disrupting compassionately becomes a gift, liberating individual voices and helping us to discern meaningful aspects of what needs to change.

Whether inside or outside a system, we can set the tone of the interaction. Imagine compassionate World Trade Organization protests. Either free or fair traders could take a first step, creating a different sort of disruption. Either could propose interacting with the "other." What could emerge if we were to delve underneath the notions of free and fair trade?

When we disrupt a system from the inside, compassion usually comes more easily. Like the editor who has to lay off 40 people, we probably know those we are disrupting. When it's personal, our hearts are more likely open to those we are disturbing.

With experience, we recognize that dissonance indicates the possibility of new and better options. Knowing that makes it easier to be curious rather than resistant or defensive. What if compassion were a guiding ideal for those plotting revolution? Nelson Mandela, Mohandas Gandhi, and Dr. Martin Luther King Jr. understood this principle. Although the systems they faced were hostile, their strategies for engaging were compassionate, applied with clear intention and commitment. And they changed their worlds. Such is the power of compassion for disrupting rigid systems.

TIPS FOR CULTIVATING COMPASSION

Because compassion is something many of us rarely contemplate, I offer some thoughts on reconnecting with your sense of compassion.

LISTEN WITH YOUR HEART. It is a good companion to the mind. Our emotional center brings a different perspective. Hear what it has to say, without judgment.

If it's been a long time since you have listened deeply to yourself, chances are there's a message backlog. It can be overwhelming at first. If so, try the following:

Create a welcoming environment for yourself before you begin.

Ask for support from a friend, a counselor, or even a workshop.

Journal. Write without judgment. And, if you wish, burn the pages when done.

FORGIVE YOURSELF AND OTHERS. Forgiveness frees energy that keeps us stuck. South Africa's Truth and Reconciliation Commission provided a remarkable space for clearing national pain and anger.

PRACTICE. It gets easier the more we do it. Ultimately, checking in with your heart feels as natural as listening to your mind. They are great partners.

DO YOUR OWN RESEARCH. Find out what works for you. A growing body of evidence suggests that compassion affects our health, productivity, and lifespan.

Practicing Compassion

My colleague Mark Jones offers the simplest practice I know for being compassionate. It is the HSLing ("hizzling") practice illustrated in Mark's story on Listening from chapter 3. The practice grew out of an audience with the Dalai Lama. The Dalai Lama told Mark that we all need to be heard, seen, and loved, or mischief occurs.

HSL stands for *h*earing, *s*eeing, and *l*oving everyone, including yourself. Mark developed a simple diagnostic:

- When people don't feel heard, they shout or shut up.
- When they don't feel seen, they get in your face and turn into bullies, or they become invisible.
- When they don't feel loved, they do a dance of approaching and avoiding—coming closer to you and then moving away.

In all cases, the remedy begins with listening. While hizzling can be used on any scale, the easiest way to start is on the scale of one to one. The next time you face a disturbance in the form of one person, join the hizzle experiment.

When Does It Make Sense to Disrupt?

Have you ever experienced or witnessed injustice? Perhaps it was on a small scale—an ethnic joke at work. Or maybe you have seen situations with constant dissonance—hostile environments, dangerous conditions, even unintended actions that trigger you in some way. Anytime we experience dissonance, we face a choice. Do we engage with it? If we suspect that staying silent means that the situation will get worse, the pressure to act increases. If we step in, we will amplify the disruption or calm it. Calming disturbance, particularly when it is emotionally charged, can suppress or ignore the deeper issues. This strategy generally results in more challenging disruptions down the road.

Of course, if we decide to amplify the disruption, that brings consequences. Engaging is never an easy decision. Yet disrupting a situation can surface useful distinctions. For example, in September 2008, when U.S. Treasury Secretary Henry Paulson appeared on television, he disrupted business as usual by making the worldwide financial crisis visible. The crisis brought unprecedented international cooperation. Given the severity of the situation, financial leaders quickly focused on a few key actions—making useful distinctions—to prevent collapse.

Distinctions that lead to breakthroughs do so because they uncover answers that meet individual needs and contribute to the larger system. Disrupting compassionately increases the likelihood of such productive consequences.

When One Person Is the Disturbance

We have all been in groups with someone who seems to poison the experience for everyone else. Perhaps he or she is always objecting or complaining or undermining the spirit of the group. Often that person has an important piece of the puzzle and lacks skill in bringing disruptive information forward in a way that others can understand it. Years ago, I was part of a management team that grew in compassion and effectiveness because one member was a constant frustration to the rest of us. We discovered the value of compassionate disruption as we learned how to work successfully with him.

He just didn't seem to fit. He was always a holdout on important decisions. No matter how much we reasoned with him, ignored him, or marginalized him, we couldn't seem to manage him out of his disruptiveness. It drove the rest of us nuts. For the longest time, we couldn't figure out what value he brought. He just got in the way. One day, I overheard some of his staff talking. I was amazed at their loyalty, their respect for him! I pointed this quality out to some of my colleagues, and our attitudes started to shift. We all admired his ability to inspire loyalty in his staff. It was a skill many of us wished we had. Now that we knew his staff loved and respected him, we had to admit that he was doing something right. We began to feel a little compassion for him. Yet on department-wide issues, we would spend precious time trying to convince him that he was wrong.

At some point, I started spending time with him one-on-one. We talked about his world—he was Latino and had grown up in a different culture than my everyone-is-Jewish-until-proved-otherwise world. As I listened, I began to respect the wisdom in his ideas. And my compassion grew. I, too, became a loyal fan. At staff meetings, when he objected, rather than joining my peers, I started to draw him out, to seek the gem of truth, the difference that made a difference, that I knew would be there. We became allies. I would ask him questions that helped us to hear what he struggled to say. Over and over, he saved us from ourselves because he knew how the staff would respond to the choices we made. We became a more compassionate management team. When disruptive decisions were necessary, we were far more conscientious in how we communicated and implemented them.

———

Most of us think, if the "problem" person would just leave, everything would be fine. While sometimes that is true, more often, if the person leaves, someone else takes her or his place. More likely, the disruptiveness is a sign that something deeper is going on. Perhaps a value or perspective is currently not welcome in the system. That one person sees it as vital to the system's health and well-being. Taking action may create dissonance, but that action is usually intended to bring value, to surface a useful distinction. If we simply react to the behavior, we miss the opportunity to learn what gifts the dissonance might contain.

My colleague taught me the value of engaging both head and heart when causing disruptions. Knowing that we may bring pain to another might cause us to want to shut down. The courage to stay open to what our hearts tell us in the moment of disrupting better equips us to discover creative distinctions that lead to emergence.

TIPS FOR DISRUPTING COHERENCE COMPASSIONATELY

Disrupting compassionately involves keeping your heart open, honoring those you are disrupting.

BE CLEAN ABOUT YOUR INTENTION. If your actions serve a greater good, proceed. If you have even a hint of ego, desire to overpower another, or want revenge, revisit your intentions.

RESPECT THOSE YOU DISRUPT. Treat others with dignity. Whatever they have done, be conscious that your actions affect them and others.

SEEK THE DIFFERENCES THAT MAKE A DIFFERENCE. Disturbance causes differences to surface. Look for the gems hidden in disruption.

A key principle:

WELCOME DISTURBANCE.

How do we find potential in the midst of disruption?

Ask possibility-oriented questions.

A key practice:

INQUIRE APPRECIATIVELY.

Asking appreciative questions is the most effective practice I know for disrupting compassionately. It interrupts the status quo so smoothly that even in challenging circumstances, those disrupted can access enthusiasm and creativity. It often finesses the feeling of disruption.

Compassionate disruption opens the way to creativity. We can help it along with a question: How do we engage disruptions creatively?

FOURTEEN

HOW DO WE ENGAGE DISRUPTIONS CREATIVELY?

Hitting is timing. Pitching is upsetting timing.

—Warren Spahn, Major League Baseball pitcher

Now that we have disrupted compassionately, it is time to engage—to fully participate with head, heart, body, and spirit. Creative interaction is at the heart of engaging emergence: connecting with ideas, each other, the system as a whole, the context in which it lives, the natural world, even ourselves. The conditions are ripe for creativity—the open-ended flow that brings novelty into being—enticing us to explore both the familiar and the unfamiliar with new eyes, or a beginner's mind, as Buddhists might say.

This chapter explores what can make disruptions creative. It points the way to the exhilarating work we encounter once we've leaped into the unknown. It offers a story of diverse people creatively engaging a disruptive challenge. It speaks to the value of embracing chaos. And it ends with tips for engaging disruptions creatively.

What Enables Disruptions to Be Creative?

When disturbed, most of us would rather hunker down someplace safe, bringing what we wish to protect with us. This attitude kills creativity. A group of us were exploring an idea for a radio show that would bring together people with different points of view in civil conversation. One person was instantly resistant. Her image was the on-air style of most talk radio: shouting matches among people with conflicting perspectives. Not exactly creative conversation. And she was not alone.

We have all experienced people interrupting each other, no one listening, everyone striving to top the other with their point of view. Nothing creative happens in that setting. If we experience only conflict when interacting with people we view as different from us, of course we'd rather find a place to hang out with our own kind. Yet we do so at the peril of our future. We need creative solutions to intractable challenges. And difference is a key ingredient.

Rather than creating a space to keep us safe and keep the other out, *creative dissonance* calls for just the opposite. Deep and essential truths often hide in dissonant behaviors like shouting or silence, bullying or invisibility. Creating conditions welcoming enough to surface these gifts enables us to use our differences creatively. As the following story about the U.S. Forest Service shows, good hosting—clear intentions, welcoming what arises, and inviting people to show up with what matters to them—fosters creative engagement.

In 2003, a coalition led by the U.S. Forest Service convened 175 diverse participants from a cross-section of communities in the San Bernardino Mountains. Trees were dying, and the Forest Service knew that fires were coming. They had prepared for the fires. While they had the public's attention, they invited residents, community associations, environmentalists, off-road-vehicle association members, business owners, ranchers, and representatives from federal, state, regional, and local governments. They gathered to envision the future, asking, "What do we want the forests to look like in 50 years?"

It was no easy task to bring together such a diverse mix. We—the Forest Service sponsors and the consulting team—formed an organizing group that included someone from each community we hoped to reach. As the members of the organizing group interacted, they discovered the creativity and value of working together. They became our voices in their communities. I suspect that none anticipated the time they would spend enticing their friends and colleagues to participate.

After months of planning, day one of the event dawned. One hundred seventy-five people from different walks of life sat at round tables of 10. All of them cared about the future of the forest. Did they trust each other? Not likely. Did they hope to have their agenda win the day? It wouldn't have surprised me.

Within the first hour, the consulting team invited people to pair up with someone different from themselves to interview each other. They were given a set of appreciative questions designed to elicit stories of what they loved about the forests and what they hoped would be there for their children. They spent the entire morning with their partners. Most came back inspired. As one man said, "I am the president of an off-road-vehicle association. I just spent the last two hours with an environmentalist. We discovered that we come to the forest for the same reason." Before we consultants could revel in our accomplishment, an older man in a cowboy hat—a rancher—stood up and essentially said that the answer to the forest's future was obvious: clear the land, sell the lumber, and let cattle graze. Even as we caught our breath from this callous declaration, no doubt intended to disrupt, we knew he was speaking for an important subset in the room that had little patience with our possibility-oriented approach.

We did a lot of soul-searching that evening, given our plans for day two. We redesigned using an analytic, left-brained activity and called it a night. At breakfast, I spoke my lingering doubts: that to back away from our original right-brained, creative activity was a mistake. We needed to trust that imaginative energies would be stirred by getting everyone out of their heads. A rich mixture of people and modalities, such as art or poetry, would lead to the best possible outcomes. My consulting partners agreed.

With trepidation, we asked participants to form groups with a mix of people from different backgrounds to create models of the forests of their desired future. We gave them crayons; small plastic toys, such as trees and people; and assorted other items. We encouraged them to play, using whatever creative forms of expression they wished to tell their story. To our surprise and relief, the "men with hats" jumped in with both feet, joining with others to envision multiuse forests that had something for everyone.

In the end, we stayed true to our intentions and didn't abandon our commitment to creativity. We welcomed the flow of life energy, even when it surfaced as derision. The artful, playful activity brought together these diverse, usually conflicted parties. The toys helped the participants to explore what mattered most. Their differences surfaced creatively. In the process, a cohesive community formed that made room for competing interests. The three-day summit resulted in a vision and principles to guide long-term decision making, a preliminary set of projects, and an ongoing committee cochaired by a government official and a community member.

Here are the principles they named:

- Key factors in land management decisions for healthy mountain ecosystems are: sustainability, biological diversity, productivity, indigenous species, resource conservation and restoration, and acknowledging fire as a natural component.

- Responsible, efficient use of natural resources promotes improved air and water quality and water quantity for the communities and natural environment.

- An open forest with healthy tree spacing supports wild lands and mountain communities that are ecologically resilient and at low risk of catastrophic wildfires.

- Care and stewardship of our mountains and forests requires education, conservation, and community involvement.

- Based on peer-reviewed science, environmental laws are stream-lined, balanced, and designed to sustain a healthy forest.

- Capacities of the mountains are recognized and understood, established and supported.

- Funding and other resources integral to the implementation of our plans are identified and available.

- Decision making is timely, inclusive, collaborative, informed, delivered, and implemented through coordinated governance.

- Responsible behavior contributes to a multiuse forest in which all living systems experience an enhanced quality of life.

This diverse group of strangers, who came together because they cared about the future of the forests, found creative answers to meet their different needs. Personal agendas gave way to common dreams of mixed-use forests that could serve today's needs and be there for great-great-grandchildren.

Benefits from Embracing Chaos

With practice, our capacity to embrace chaos expands. We learn to tolerate the absence of guiding principles that bring order to our situation. Think about driving in another country. The assumptions about how traffic works in India are unlike those in the United States. It takes 360-degree vision to navigate among the chaotic flow of cars, bicycles, mule-drawn carts, and other vehicles. Horn honks are friendly signals meaning someone is behind you, rather than the angry sound of "Get out of my way." Driving in another culture requires letting go of familiar rules of traffic flow and opening to learning how to drive anew. I love finding meaning in unfamiliar aspects, such as mule carts backing up on a main street, and discovering new meaning in old aspects, such as horns.

We learn to use our differences creatively. As our different perspectives rub against each other, a burnishing occurs. Together, we make meaning, uncovering patterns that draw from what each of us brings. Expressing our differences carries the seeds of what might be. When conditions enable us all to show up and engage fully, warts and all, what is most meaningful shines through, over and over. We become a "differentiated wholeness" in which our unique gifts weave together into a coherent tapestry. Think of a championship basketball team at the top of its game. Every player brings what she or he does best. Together, they create something of beauty, grace, and power. In that moment, there's no room for egos. Yet each player is great, contributing to the larger good. No one is alone. They are part of a whole.

In the midst of creative disruption, hearts open and we discover that we are connected. In truth, even when we can't feel it because our hearts are closed, we are still connected. Just as head, heart, hands, and other parts connect to form our body, our unique gifts connect us into a larger, creative social body.

Creative engagement isn't without angst. During a 2009 Journalism That Matters gathering, I sat in on a deep conversation about what mainstream journalists cherished. I finally understood that some of the fear and grief many expressed was over the possibility that enduring values of journalism, such as accuracy and transparency, would be swept away. What, in fact, became clear during the session was that such values are essential to conserve as so much else changes. Ironically, new technologies provide tools for even greater accuracy and transparency. What matters endures. New forms can amplify deeper intentions. As we discover our place in the mix, excitement builds, possibilities abound, and we creatively find answers together. As one journalist put it, when systems break down, you gather up the pieces and make something new. Simple, though not easy. The next question—how do we renew coherence wisely?—sheds light on how.

TIPS FOR ENGAGING DISRUPTIONS CREATIVELY

WHEN FEELING OVERWHELMED, BREATHE. Chaotic settings are stressful. Catching our breath helps us to reconnect with ourselves.

PAY ATTENTION. If you can't see the guiding patterns, listen, observe, and be receptive to what surrounds you. Notice what is meaningful. Make an intuitive inventory of what is happening.

BRING A BEGINNER'S MIND. Look at the familiar with new eyes. Is it still meaningful? Is it something to conserve? What is new and unexpected? Look through the eyes of someone who finds excitement in it. Is it something to be embraced?

Key principles:

PIONEER!

How do we discover our way forward?

Seek new directions. Think different. Break a habit. Act courageously.

ENCOURAGE RANDOM ENCOUNTERS.

How do we create conditions in which chance interactions among diverse members of a system lead to breakthroughs?

Widen the circle of participation. Invite the diverse members of the system to take responsibility for what they love as an act of service.

A key practice:

TAKE RESPONSIBILITY FOR WHAT YOU LOVE AS AN ACT OF SERVICE.

This practice liberates our hearts, minds, and spirits, calling us to put our unique gifts to use. The more it becomes an operating norm, the more innovation, joy, solidarity, generosity, and other qualities of well-being appear. It is the essence of engaging disruptions creatively.

FIFTEEN

HOW DO WE RENEW COHERENCE WISELY?

The act of sense making is discovering new terrain as you are making it.

—Brian Arthur, economist, Santa Fe Institute

Remember Humpty Dumpty's fall? The pieces didn't fit together again. Emergence is like that. What arises from creative interactions is not a return to former times. It is more of a spiral, a re-newal—new again. Some elements circle around from the past. Others are original. Together, they form something novel and of a higher-order complexity.

This chapter explores coherence, the last aspect of change's pattern of disturbing, differentiating, and coalescing. It opens with a story of differences cohering. It reflects on renewal and wisdom. It talks of the nature of networks, which are showing up as an emerging form for how we organize our systems. It ends with tips for renewing coherence wisely.

The Spirit of Renewal

When we're in the midst of creative disruptions, what helps our work come to fruition? What enables a higher-order understanding to coalesce? Reflecting, inviting people to share their stories, and naming what has heart and meaning helps to surface what hides in our midst.

Beginning with individual energy, coherence arises from the inside out. Unlike puzzle pieces mechanically connecting, new forms arise almost magically out of our interactions. They coalesce as differences intersect. People share what matters to them, they interact and influence each other, and a handful of themes invariably surface. Something is named that lands deeply and broadly. People carry it to others struggling to find their way. Although days, months, or years may pass before it is widely embraced, something is different. Something new has been born into the world.

The Journalism That Matters story below describes how novel ideas arise in our social systems. It happens not through assembling the parts, but through a more nuanced reformation that involves random interactions coalescing in unpredictable ways.

A 2009 Journalism That Matters event is under way. The conference room, awash with the warmth of the Florida sun, is awhirl with activity. A question has been posed to focus the gathering: What is our work in the new news ecology?

A diverse mix of mainstream journalists, technologists, new media people, educators, reformers, and others set their agenda:

- Who funds investigative reporting?
- What do we teach our journalism students?
- How does social media affect journalism?
- What's the role of humor in journalism?
- Are we having fun yet?

People self-organize around the topics they have chosen. They pursue the conversations that matter to them. An activist expresses her frustration with finding investigative reporters willing to listen. The reporters coach her on how to get their attention. By the end of the conversation, they each see the other differently, appreciating the challenges and constraints of each other's worlds.

Angst and fear of what will happen as newspapers die gives way to an undercurrent of excitement and possibility. Opportunities are showing up everywhere. Stories surface of community-hosted sites where the audience is part of the investigative process and journalists are "writing in public." Journalism curriculum is reimagined to include media literacy for everyone, traditional values and craft, and the emerging art of engagement—cultivating civil conversation online and face-to-face in a geographic or subject-oriented community. A myriad of possibilities are explored, ideas surfaced.

A sorting takes place, as aspects of the past, present, and future are tasted and embraced or discarded. Through random engagement, following the energy and passion of the people present, the system is examined in depth. Questions are asked, debated, mourned, and celebrated: What still has meaning that we wish to conserve? What do we wish to embrace that is possible because of changes in technology or attitudes?

It is the last morning. People sit together in a circle. They arrived as strangers. Now they sit comfortably with each other, joking over the angst that surfaced more than once during their time together. They glimpsed the future and found it promising. Most feel full, inspired by ideas they are taking home. They know they are in good company with kindred spirits who care about the future of journalism. They have partners in shaping that future. They are part of something larger—the rebirth of an industry, a calling that serves the public good. They begin telling a new story of journalism, more conversation than lecture, more entrepreneurial and nimble. It seems more resilient, with room for more voices. Cooperation increases. People know they are connected, part of the same system, all pursuing what matters to them, sharing what they have learned, figuring it out together.

In some ways, nothing has changed. The economics of journalism are as murky as when the participants arrived. They may be going home to lay off people or to take a buyout. In other ways, everything has changed. Most feel more at peace with not knowing the answers. Joan Baez is quoted frequently: "Action is the antidote to despair." No longer victims of the unknown, they see their own next step. And they now know others traveling a similar path, partners in exploration and learning.

A network of pioneers is forming. At root, journalism's fundamental purpose endures—to inform, inspire, and activate for the public good. New technology makes it possible to involve more people in serving this mission. So, something novel and of a higher-order form is emerging. Clearly, journalism is no longer in the hands of a few people. Complex networks of professionals, para-professionals, and an engaged public are part of the budding scene. Its shape is far from clear. It will likely be that way for a while. Journalism is between stories, transitioning from old forms to new, more adaptive forms. The holy grail of a sustainable business model may not yet be known, but these people are now pioneers on the trail, inventing the future.

———————————

Journalism is in the midst of renewing itself, finding its way to what matters now. Such is the way of coherence: people catch glimpses of what is arising and more experiments are seeded, accelerating the process as they carry the harvest home with them.

A turn on a spiral of change happens as something thoroughly original and elegantly complex also embodies enduring needs and values. It defies tidy descriptions as new and old aspects intertwine in the dance of differentiating and coalescing. Evolution itself is under way, sometimes incrementally, sometimes making unexpected leaps. Literally meaning "to make new again," renewal contains what endures, a return to our deepest needs, intentions, and values. Renewal also holds what wasn't possible before: novel forms. Innovations like Twitter find their relationship to existing forms of journalism. Every once in a while, something flips and becomes a new organizing principle. For example, journalism is entrepreneurial. It begins the process of reorganizing everything. The printing press opened the way to the 19th-century mass literacy movement.[1] Today, media literacy follows the need to discern quality in the multiple sources that make up new forms of journalism. When we reorganize ourselves around emerging principles, bringing order to a more diverse, complex system, the transition keeps us busy!

Cultivating Wise Renewal

Has something wise been realized? Chances are, we won't know for a while. At root, *wisdom* means "to see, to know the way." Knowledge or knowing arises from and serves the whole. Such knowledge and knowing is deeper than the rational mind. It includes intuitions forged through experience.

In a wise society, people continually grow their capacity to care for themselves, each other, and the whole. Institutions are designed to support this growth. For example, the U.S. Constitution is a living promise, an elegant set of principles that exemplifies wise renewal. What "We the people" means continues to evolve. Sometimes it happens through violent disruption, like the Civil War. Sometimes it occurs through more compassionate disruptions, like the women's suffrage. Both influenced social attitudes and legal action. Ultimately, constitutional amendments abolished slavery and gave women the vote. African-Americans became whole people, rather than three-fifths of a person, as slaves were counted in the Constitution. More recently, Ecuador has led the way to including nature's rights in its new constitution. With nature's needs appearing in such a foundational document, a deeper innate wisdom is coalescing.

Wisdom seems to be emerging more often as evolution itself evolves toward increasing complexity, diversity, and awareness. Whether truth and reconciliation in South Africa or peace in Northern Ireland, intractable challenges are being settled peacefully. Perhaps wise renewal is moving us toward increased energy efficiency. Emergence through creative engagement no doubt uses far less energy than war.

The capacity to engage diverse perspectives creatively may be the evolutionary leap that our current social and environmental crises are forcing. Handling so much complexity wisely means that we can't do it alone. Although wisdom may be expressed through an individual, it is not a solo act. It involves our relationships with each other and our environment. Wisdom lives in the collective. Knowing how to bring together difference and stay connected is a critical skill for our times. Hosting productive conversations among increasingly diverse people is part of a new story of who we are as a society. The Internet gives us an unprecedented lens into other cultures. Social networking capabilities are rapidly increasing our ability to interact. How we use these opportunities is up to us. This is a good time to learn more about wisdom. As a consultant colleague, Martin Rutte, says, "You have to do it by yourself. And you can't do it alone."

At our wisest, we know to sense in many directions—inside and outside the boundaries of a system, from the tangible and intangible, from the individual and collective. We use many ways of knowing, listening to the mind, the heart, the body—including the social body—and the spirit.

What seems wise in one age or circumstance may seem foolish in another. There is a Taoist story: One day, a farmer's horse ran away, and all the neighbors gathered in the evening and said, "That's too bad." He said, "Maybe." Next day, the horse came back and brought with it seven wild horses. "Wow!" said the Taoist villagers, "aren't you lucky!" He said, "Maybe." The next day, his son tried to saddle-train one of the wild horses. The son was thrown and broke his leg. And all the neighbors said. "Oh, that's too bad." The farmer said, "Maybe." The next day, the conscription officers came around, gathering young men for the army. They rejected the man's son because he had a broken leg. And the villagers all came around and said, "Isn't that great! Your son got out." He said, "Maybe." And the story continues.

With wisdom comes patience, continually reflecting, staying open to what is emerging as others rush to judgment. That said, since humans are involved, we'll undoubtedly try a wealth of experiments, some wise, some not so wise. If an innovation creates disruption, it indicates that something is attracting interest. Someone or something excluded cares enough to make it known. We circle back to disrupting compassionately, knowing that welcoming the outside in brings treasures. In this way, perhaps a bit more wisdom grows.

Networks Emerging

It is a good time for wisdom because we are, in fact, in the midst of renewing how we organize ourselves for just about everything we do. Technology and changing perspectives make hierarchies and rigid structures less critical. The notion of leader as heroic individual is losing its shine. Networks, more adaptive and resilient, are slowly taking their place, along with the understanding that leaders are everywhere, in each of us.

For example, Wikipedia is a terrific place to follow breaking news. As a story unfolds, those closest to it add or correct information, and link to photos or other Web sites for details. Filtering facts happens through self-correcting crowdsourcing. We no longer depend on a few professionals for all aspects of the story. Leadership arises as people within the situation answer some internal call to serve, taking responsibility for what they love. While the need for information continues, it is served through an original means: a network of engaged strangers.

In all sorts of systems, networks of conversations are replacing the old forms—ink on paper, gatekeepers telling us what we need to know, and so on. In spite of itself, journalism is leading the way, providing hints of what's to come for a variety of our social systems. News and information are now delivered to a mix of devices—computers, televisions, iPods—as well as ink on paper. Hierarchies are giving way to networks. Single points of control for story ideas, follow-up information, accuracy, and other aspects yield to networks better able to handle complexity that is impossible to address any other way. Habits from one form are revisited both practically and emotionally. Technology helps us to operate more fluidly. Yet for those of us who didn't grow up as digital natives, it can be daunting!

What does it take to function well in a network? We are novices at this. Increasing numbers of us are experimenting, most without consciously knowing we are part of a great reordering. Some of us disrupt more compassionately, use our differences creatively, and renew wisely. We are sharing the results in creative ways—through Facebook, YouTube, Twitter, and other forms that make visible our interconnectedness. A virtuous cycle is forming in which more and more of us can see our place in a multistoried world that has room for us all. Perhaps some additional seeds of wisdom live in that more nuanced view.

Networks are children of emergence. They turn what we know about how organizations work inside out. Rather than rigid boundaries defining them, clear intentions are the glue binding networks together. Rather than assigned leaders, people and organizations step in, taking responsibility for what they love. Some become hubs, attracting others to them. They are relational leaders, whose influence derives from the depth and breadth of their connections. Guiding principles emerge as people take responsibility for resolving disruptions.

We know that networks are highly collaborative. Leadership shifts fluidly as work groups form and disperse as needed. Networks also provide a different relationship with context—knowing how we fit with others and our environment.

When we experience ourselves as part of a larger system, something profound happens: our behavior changes. This turning point is a crowning moment of wise renewal. We realize that to ignore or harm another part of our social body—or our ecological body—would be like cutting off our own arm. Disruption indicates that something we thought was outside the system wants in. A bit wiser, we may even meet the disturbance with curiosity.

TIPS FOR RENEWING COHERENCE WISELY

SURFACE WHAT MATTERS TO EACH ASPECT OF THE SYSTEM. Coherence arises when diversity is welcome. Not all differences are significant. Seek what is at the heart of the differences.

TRUST THAT USEFUL OUTCOMES CAN ARISE. Let go of needing immediate answers. Coherence is not constructed. Don't treat the aspects of a system like puzzle pieces. Doing so generally suboptimizes outcomes and leaves unhappy people in its wake.

BE PREPARED TO BE SURPRISED. We can do our best to create conditions that make emergence more likely. Once it is set in motion, how, when, and why it happens and what specifically emerges is an unexpected leap. The magic lives in the unlikely, unlooked-for connections.

Key principles:

SEEK MEANING.

How do we surface what matters to individuals and to the whole?

Be receptive. Suspend the desire for closure. Ask reflective questions. Have faith that meaning arises.

SIMPLIFY.

What is the least we need to do to create the most benefit?

Continually seek the essence at the heart of what matters.

A key practice:

REFLECT.

Sense patterns. Get curious about what is arising. Ask questions that tease out what is surfacing. Name it, harvest the stories, and share them widely.

I said in the introduction that change is too important to leave solely in the hands of professionals. By now, I expect that you feel better equipped to engage with disruption in the systems in which you live and work. Whether it's family, work, community, or another system of which you are a part, step in. In the pages that follow, I offer you some closing thoughts and challenges as you do.

WHAT'S POSSIBLE NOW?

Every new beginning comes from some
other beginning's end.

—Seneca, Roman philosopher and statesman

It is a funny thing about our cultural stories. We seem to tell more of them that reinforce our belief in collapsing systems than ones that inspire a belief in renewing systems. Stories of breakdown are everywhere. We find them in newspapers, in magazines, on TV, in movies, and on the Internet. We know that ecosystems flourish, collapse, and arise anew over time. So do social systems. They rise up, become "too big to fail," and weaken, even as something new takes shape. New beginnings are all around us. Yet they become visible only when we ask questions focused on possibility.

A renewal is under way, a modern renaissance fueled by the passion and commitment of many who have dared to pursue a dream. In communities, organizations, industries, and other social systems, stories of new ways of living and working are flourishing. They are visible if we simply choose to look for them. Some people and organizations are beginning to do just that. And they are sharing the stories, making this rebirth more apparent to all of us, inspiring more of us to engage.

These closing reflections are a call to act. They invite each of us to engage emergence. I offer some suggestions in these final pages for ways to compassionately disrupt, creatively engage, and wisely renew the systems we all share. I end by describing a promising approach for taking our capacity to engage emergence to scale. *Macroscopes*—tools that make complexity visible—are a means to reach a turning point in the larger emergence we are collectively experiencing. Just as the dashboard on our car helps us to drive safely, imagine technologies that help us to understand far more complex systems, like power grids or the state of health care. Such is the promise of macroscopes.

Get Involved

This book is about equipping us to work with upheaval and change. It provides *practices*, *principles*, and *questions* for engaging emergence. So let us put these notions to work. We can be part of that renaissance. I begin with three requests:

- Be compassionate disrupters, asking possibility-oriented questions and telling stories of rebirth.

- Creatively engage, interacting with people outside our comfort zone.

- Support wise renewal, seeking more nuanced perspectives that help us to see ourselves in context.

Compassionately Disrupt

We have an important opportunity to shed light on the renaissance that is under way. This renaissance is engaging millions of people around the world. The more of us asking questions that spark possibilities, the more that renaissance spreads. Even as many of our systems are collapsing, something extensively covered by the media, we are in the midst of a quiet rebirth.

We can disrupt our way to a virtuous cycle of creativity and renewal. If you are skeptical, consider these indicators that something important is happening:

- Paul Hawken's *Blessed Unrest: How the Largest Movement in the World Came into Being and Why No One Saw It Coming* is a testament to what has germinated in the dark soils of despair.[1] Hawken describes a convergence of environmental, indigenous, and social justice movements as the largest social movement in history. This movement, he says, is also the fastest growing movement ever, including more than a million organizations from every country in the world.

- A journalism colleague, Deborah Brandt, was stunned when she began researching stories of transformative change. She found hundreds simply because she started looking. She concludes her research: "[C]onsidering the volume of information and activity around this [change] movement, it warrants its own regular coverage. This movement is spreading through every area, including business, educational, economic, environmental, and spiritual development. Futurists tell us that this century will produce change ten times faster than in the last century."[2]

Ironically, journalists can start with telling their own story. Journalism is being reborn, grounded in the deep desire to serve the public good that originally drew most journalists I have met into the field. Through the power of technology, they are discovering that it is more possible today than ever before to deliver on their essential purpose of informing, inspiring, engaging, and activating people to be self-governing. Innovations are everywhere. The scale is currently small, but a thousand flowers are definitely blooming. Is journalism fragmented and chaotic? Absolutely. Do we have a clear answer yet? Not by a long shot. But we are learning and sharing rapidly. A viable model will likely be dynamic, be possibility-oriented, and create an interactive relationship between journalist and community. When such a model coalesces, we will wonder how we could have missed an obvious solution.

Having come through the eye of the storm, journalists will be well equipped to share the story of collapse and rebirth. They can help us all to understand how to apply what they learn about disrupting compassionately, engaging creatively, and renewing wisely. Of course, it isn't just journalism.

Whatever field of endeavor you are in, look around. The seeds are everywhere. Be willing to be the disruptive force in your world. Do it compassionately, of course. Welcome the disturbances around you. Use them to inspire you to pioneer, to engage the possibilities inherent in the loosening of old habits.

Creatively Engage

The more we reach beyond our usual friends and colleagues to engage others, the more potential there is for creative outcomes. Get curious about something. Ask yourself a question and be playful with it. Set up your own random encounters. Go someplace you don't ordinarily go. Talk with people you rarely meet. Engage with an assumption that something good can come of it, and seek it out.

Be part of the media. Since journalists are no longer the sole arbiters of meaning, we all have a role in being the voices of possibility, sharing stories of our cultural renewal. In communities throughout the world, both geographic and interest based, ordinary people are becoming a new breed of journalists. They report on their neighborhood or field. Many create online communities that provide a place to get involved. If a place to gather doesn't exist in your area, start one. Meet your neighbors.

Be a compassionate voice of possibility in settings that are fixated on what's wrong. You know what to do. Break the habit that too many of us have, of focusing on what's wrong. Ask some variant of "Given all of that, what's possible now?"

Cultivate space for creative engagement. Honor different perspectives, seeking their gifts rather than making them wrong. Since we don't know which interactions will catalyze a coming together, help create conditions for a myriad of encounters. Listen for what is emerging. Revel in being part of the renewal.

If, like many of us, you're too busy to start something, then look for the opportunities that show up day to day. Negativity and despair are all around. When you hear them, find the compassion in you to engage creatively. Ask a question of possibility. Maybe you are standing in line at the grocery store or in the silence of an elevator ride. When you overhear a complaint, ask a friendly question. Perhaps, "What do you really want?" Or "What would it look like if it were working?" Take a stand for connection in a time of separation. You never know the difference it can make.

Wisely Renew

As you engage, notice the threads of meaning that surface. Reflect on what has energy, and name what you sense coming together. Seek the simplicity that arises when tensions coalesce into something novel. But be patient. If you're working hard to find the pattern, chances are it is too soon. Give it time to steep, even if the mystery is uncomfortable. Find something to enjoy about the engagement itself, the creative exploration of possibilities, to ease your impatience. Wisdom has this annoying way of arising only after you've let go of needing to know now.

Seek meaning by making connections visible. New technologies are helping us to find patterns, making complexity understandable. Search for that understanding, particularly when the situation is multifaceted or conflicted.

Imagine a map of the million-plus organizations that Paul Hawken names in *Blessed Unrest*. What if that map lets us see what's available in our own backyard and how it relates to other communities, organizations, and activities around the world? Suddenly, we have a highly contextualized understanding of how we all fit together and where each of us can make a difference.

The Promise of the Macroscope

A turning point occurs when we experience ourselves as part of something larger. Perhaps our voice rises in harmony with others. Or we have overcome an obstacle because we used our different skills and abilities to accomplish something together that none of us could have done alone. We change through such experiences. They break through habits of separation that keep us fragmented. Our personal stories become a doorway into the universal. We find ourselves undeniably interconnected, even with those we never saw as part of "us" before.

When people all over the globe viewed our world with no boundaries from space, we experienced ourselves anew. For many of us, this first sight of the Earth from space made visceral what we all knew in the abstract: political borders are human creations. We knew we were

"The Blue Marble"[3]

connected. Slowly, quietly, this insight triggered an unstoppable journey toward a more respectful relationship with the Earth and among people of all cultures.

Emergent change processes create this experience of being part of a larger whole for tens, hundreds, sometimes thousands of people. While it may change those directly involved, how does it scale? How can we reach that turning point with millions or billions of us?

Technologies—from meditation to the Internet—can amplify our ability to sense how we belong. They can help us to harvest the stories in novel, creative ways. They can bring into broad awareness what we are learning about working well with disruption and difference.

Joel de Rosnay, author of *The Symbiotic Man*, introduced the notion of the macroscope.[4] Just as microscopes help us to see the infinitely small and telescopes help us to see the infinitely large, macroscopes help us to see the infinitely complex. Rather than a single instrument, they are a class of tools for sensing complex interconnections among information, ideas, people, and experiences. Maps, stories, art, media, or some combination of them all could be used as macroscopic tools that would help us to see ourselves in a larger context. For example, consider the brilliant use of technology in a baseball stadium. We are able to experience the game from many angles. At a glance, the scoreboard tells us the state of play. Cameras zoom in so that we can see the action not just on the field but also in the audience. Television dramatically extends the reach of the event. And a history of statistics available online lets both professional commentators and ordinary people put the activities in perspective. We can immerse ourselves in the experience and understand it from many perspectives. Imagine applying such thoughtfulness to making the state of the economy, education, or a war visible to us all.

Both microscopes and telescopes sparked tremendous innovation. Macroscopes have such potential today. They help us to see ourselves in relationship—how we fit with each other and our environment. Because this experience changes our fundamental sense of who we are, macroscopes could be instrumental in helping us to coalesce, surfacing wise, shared meaning out of the disruptions plaguing so many of our systems today.

Imagine: What if we could easily see a range of perspectives? More than side A or B, for or against, what does the nuanced landscape of multiple perspectives on any issue—health care reform, abortion, gay marriage—look like? How do different populations, ages, functions, ethnicities look at it? What if we had the tools to make this information visible? Those tools are coming.

In the spirit of the macroscope, people are creating a myriad of approaches to harvesting stories that enable us see how our diverse cultural narratives fit together. These Web sites, movies, games, and other media help us to see complexity. They change our understanding of who and what is outside and inside a system. The tools are young but taking shape quickly.

For example, the Sunlight Foundation uses cutting-edge technology to make government transparent and accountable.[5] One project, OpenGov Tracker, aggregates data from multiple sources to make visible the levels of transparency, participation, collaboration, and innovation in U.S. government agencies.[6] Imagine coupling the Sunlight Foundation's database sophistication with the beautiful visualization tools from Digg—a place for people to discover and share content from anywhere on the Web.[7]

Such tools will challenge us to develop the skills to bring information to life. They will help us to tell stories through which we experience our differences as creative potential for a wiser, more compassionate society. And the time is none too soon!

As change accelerates, we are well served to understand the effect of our human footprint in both space and time. What would it mean if we could see the speed with which we are using the natural resources of our planet? Would we behave differently if we experienced how interconnected we really are? Creating such contextualized views, seeing coherent maps of how we fit together, engages us deeply—mentally, emotionally, and spiritually. Context helps us to act locally, informed by a higher order and more global perspective. It can also energize us through generating a gut understanding that we are all in it together. The tools can provide faster, more visible feedback loops with which to understand the consequences of our choices.

New forms of journalism and other types of storytellers are experimenting with these capabilities. For example, Minnesota Public Radio created an online game that the public could play to balance the state budget.[8] Not only did people learn more about the challenging trade-offs, but legislators were able to see what mattered to their constituents.

The more stories we harvest that make sense of how our different perspectives fit together, the more we start internalizing a "macroscopic" view—acting from understanding the complex relationships that make us a system. We coalesce at a higher order of complexity, network upon network of interrelated individuals who together form a differentiated, yet coherent, whole.

As we appreciate our interconnectedness, our sense of who is our community expands. The conditions for more trust and courage emerge. We act, knowing something about the collective assumptions and intentions we share. We become clearer about our own work and how we connect with others. New insights, partnerships, and initiatives emerge. Ultimately, we may experience ourselves as being of the Earth, not just on it, which would catalyze a radical shift in the story we tell ourselves about our place in the universe.

When we harvest shared stories big enough to contain us all, something quite new will have emerged on this planet. We are calling into being our collective soul so that our many-storied world can find its way, and each of us our paths through it. And a new cultural narrative is reshaping who we are.

Will it be enough? It is impossible to predict. But given that we know what will happen if we continue on the existing path, why not proceed?

So, go ahead. Walk the path that gives you energy, compassionately disrupting as you go. Keep the flame ablaze for what holds meaning as you join with others to creatively engage, even though you may
never know all the good you do. Together, we can help wisdom rise
anew. I'll see you along the way.

SIMPLE WAYS TO GET INVOLVED

Grow your capacity to engage emergence. Keep stepping up your
game, with increasingly complex challenges and diverse groups.

ASK POSSIBILITY-ORIENTED QUESTIONS. Be a champion for the
appreciative. Especially in unlikely places, inquire into what is working, what is possible given what's happening.

INTERACT WITH PEOPLE OUTSIDE YOUR COMFORT ZONE. Discover
how stimulating it is to experience difference. In the process, you
may develop some unexpected partnerships for bringing together
diverse groups who care about the same issues.

SEEK MORE NUANCED PERSPECTIVES THAT HELP US TO SEE OUR-
SELVES IN CONTEXT. If you are faced with A-versus-B choices, open
up the exploration. Seek out other points of view. Discover the
deeper meaning that connects deeply felt needs.

TELL STORIES OF UPHEAVAL TURNED TO OPPORTUNITY. Help take
to scale what's possible when you engage emergence. Share your
experiences of working with disruption. Explore using tools that
offer a macroscopic view to expand your reach.

SUMMARY OF KEY IDEAS

History will be kind to me for I intend to write it.

—Sir Winston Churchill

A Pattern of Change

- **DIFFERENTIATION** teases apart useful distinctions:

  What do we wish to conserve?

  What do we wish to embrace that wasn't possible before?

- **COHERENCE** arises as disparate aspects cluster to create a complex, novel whole.

- **DISRUPTION** interrupts habitual activity.

Forms of Change

In order of increasing disruption:

STEADY STATE—Disturbance is handled within the existing situation. A minor fix is made, or the disruption is ignored or suppressed. Business as usual continues. For example: a speeder gets a ticket for driving too fast.

INCREMENTAL SHIFTS—Disruptions interrupt the status quo. We distinguish what the disturbance brings to the system and integrate changes. For example: an existing constitution is amended following protests that spark legal action.

EMERGENCE—Occasional upheaval results when principles that keep a system orderly break down. Chaos sparks

191

experiments. Current assumptions are clarified, and new possibilities surface. Ultimately, something dies, and a new coherence arises that contains aspects of the old and the new but isn't either. For example: a revolution leads to a new form of governance.

Benefits of Engaging Emergence

INDIVIDUALLY, WE ARE STRETCHED AND REFRESHED. We feel more courageous and inspired to pursue what matters to us.

NEW AND UNLIKELY PARTNERSHIPS FORM. When we connect with people whom we don't normally meet, sparks can fly. Creative conditions make room for our differences, fostering lively and productive interactions.

BREAKTHROUGH PROJECTS SURFACE. Experiments are inspired by interactions among diverse people.

COMMUNITY IS STRENGTHENED. We discover kindred spirits among a diverse mix of strangers. Lasting connections form, and a sense of kinship grows.

THE CULTURE CHANGES. With time and continued interaction, a new narrative of who we are takes shape.

Some Catches When Engaging Emergence

- Getting started is a leap of faith.
- Success can be a hurdle.
- Outcomes can be elusive to recognize.
- What's most important is likely not on our radar screen.
- Not everyone makes the trip.
- Death or loss is usually part of the mix.

Characteristics of Emergence

RADICAL NOVELTY—At each level of complexity, entirely new properties appear—for example, from autocracy (rule by one person with unlimited power) to democracy (people are the ultimate source of political power).

COHERENCE—A stable system of interactions (for example, elephant, biosphere, agreement).

WHOLENESS—Not just the sum of its parts, but also different and irreducible from its parts (for example, humans are more than the composition of lots of cells).

DYNAMIC—Always in process, continuing to evolve (for example, changes in transportation: walking, horse and buggy, autos, trains, buses, airplanes, and so on).

DOWNWARD CAUSATION—The system shaping the behavior of the parts (for example, roads determine where we drive).

Dynamics of Emergence

SITUATIONAL LEADERSHIP ARISING IN CONTEXT. Generally characterized as no one being in charge. Or everyone being in charge. In fact, what's in charge is the energy of the situation and of the people taking initiative, interacting in it.

SIMPLE RULES ENGENDER COMPLEX BEHAVIOR. Randomness becomes coherent as individuals, each following a few basic principles or assumptions, interact with their neighbors.

FEEDBACK AMONG NEIGHBORING AGENTS. Interactions that reinforce and balance the system. Reinforcing feedback loops encourage action in the same general direction—sometimes toward more, sometimes toward less. They are sometimes called vicious or, when in a healthy direction, virtuous cycles.

Balancing feedback loops are opposite forces responsively interacting, as needed, to counter each other, creating a dynamic stable state.

CLUSTERING AS LIKE FINDS LIKE. Diverse agents interact, feeding back to each other. Some individual agents bond around a shared characteristic, forming more complex systems, such as networks, over time.

Questions for Engaging Emergence

- How do we disrupt coherence compassionately?
- How do we engage disruptions creatively?
- How do we renew coherence wisely?

Principles for Engaging Emergence

WELCOME DISTURBANCE.
How do we find potential in the midst of disruption?
Ask possibility-oriented questions.

PIONEER!
How do we discover our way forward?
Seek new directions. Think different. Break a habit. Act courageously.

ENCOURAGE RANDOM ENCOUNTERS.
How do we create conditions in which chance interactions among diverse members of a system lead to breakthroughs?
Widen the circle of participation. Invite the diverse members of the system to take responsibility for what they love as an act of service.

SEEK MEANING.

How do we surface what matters to individuals and to the whole?

Be receptive. Suspend the desire for closure. Ask reflective questions. Have faith that meaning arises.

SIMPLIFY.

What is the least we need to do to create the most benefit?

Continually seek the essence at the heart of what matters.

Practices for Engaging Emergence

Step Up

How do we engage so that we achieve the best possible outcomes?

TAKE RESPONSIBILITY FOR WHAT YOU LOVE AS AN ACT OF SERVICE.

How can we use our differences and commonalities to make a difference?

Get involved with what matters, listening and connecting along the way.

LISTEN: SENSE BROADLY AND DEEPLY, WITNESSING WITH SELF DISCIPLINE.

How do we more fully understand each other and our environment?

Pay attention using all of our senses to learn and adapt.

CONNECT: BRIDGE DIFFERENCES AND BOND WITH OTHERS.

How do we link ourselves and our ideas with others similar to and different from ourselves?

Listen for deeper meaning to seek common ground.

Prepare

How do we equip ourselves to engage disturbance?

EMBRACE MYSTERY: SEEK THE GIFTS HIDDEN IN WHAT WE DON'T KNOW.

What does it take to be receptive to the unknown?
Let go of the need for immediate answers.

CHOOSE POSSIBILITY: CALL FORTH "WHAT COULD BE."

What do we want more of?
Seek positive guiding images.

FOLLOW LIFE ENERGY: TRUST DEEPER SOURCES OF DIRECTION.

What guides us when we don't know?
Work with the energies that are present.

Host

How do we steward what is arising among us?

FOCUS INTENTIONS: CLARIFY OUR CALLING.

What purpose moves us?
Tune in. Sense what is stirring in ourselves, others, and our environment.

WELCOME: CULTIVATE HOSPITABLE SPACE.

How do we cultivate conditions for the best possible outcomes?
Create a spirit of welcome—physically, socially, intellectually, emotionally, and spiritually.

INVITE THE DIVERSITY OF THE SYSTEM.

How can we include the true complexity of the situation?
Reach out to those who ARE IN: with authority, resources, expertise, information, and need.

Engage

How do we engage emergence?

INQUIRE APPRECIATIVELY: ASK BOLD QUESTIONS OF POSSIBILITY.

How do we inspire explorations that lead to positive action?

Ask questions that focus toward a positive intention, and invite others to engage with us.

OPEN: BE RECEPTIVE.

How do we make space for the whole story—good, bad, or indifferent?

Be willing to be more in questions than answers.

REFLECT: SENSE PATTERNS, BE A MIRROR.

What is arising now?

Get curious. Ask questions that tease out what is coming into being. Be a witness for another.

NAME: MAKE MEANING.

How do we call forth what is ripening?

Be receptive to a leap that can come from anywhere.

HARVEST: SHARE STORIES.

Once meaning is named, how does it spread?

Tell the stories. Write, draw, sing, dance, etc. Capture the spirit in print, video, online, and other media. Since we absorb more through multiple forms of expression, the more media, the better.

Iterate

DO IT AGAIN: CONTINUE TO EVOLVE.

What keeps us going?

Integrate what we know into what's novel and what's novel into what we know.

Emergence in Context

- Emergent novelty arises in occasional discontinuous leaps.

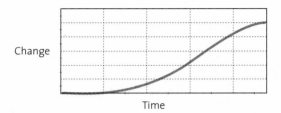

- Novelty is internalized incrementally over time as we weave together what's new and what we know, establishing new operating principles (simple rules).

    » It starts slow.

    » Its evolution is nonlinear.

    » It spirals over the long sweep of time, returning to the same place, but different.

- Sustainability arises as new operating principles (simple rules) that work well in the new conditions are widely integrated into a system.

- Resilient social systems are well served by stewarding shared intention and tending to the social fabric of a system. They have the following:

    » A guiding image of a desirable future

    » Mutual support

    » An interactive, transparent communications infrastructure

    » Capacity for hosting conversations that matter

    » Capacity to engage emergence when disruptions occur

The Promise of the Macroscope

- A turning point occurs when we experience ourselves as part of a larger system.

- Harming another part of our social body—or our ecological body—is like cutting off an arm.

- When we know we are connected, we use our diverse skills and abilities to accomplish what none of us can do on our own.

- Macroscopes hold promise for scaling our work through creative use of technology.

Simple Ways to Get Involved

- Ask possibility-oriented questions.

- Interact with people outside your comfort zone.

- Seek more nuanced perspectives that help us to see ourselves in context.

- Tell stories of upheaval turned to opportunity.

ABOUT EMERGENT
CHANGE PROCESSES

I will not follow where the path may
lead, but I will go where there is no path,
and I will leave a trail.

—Muriel Strode, *My Little Book of Prayer*

Emergent change processes engage the diverse people of a system in focused yet open interactions that lead to unexpected and lasting shifts in perspective and behavior.

The roots of these processes grew out of three traditions: social psychology, psychoanalytic theory, and systems theory.[1] Perhaps the earliest experiment that united these threads by involving people in changing their own systems occurred in 1960. Social scientists Fred Emery and Eric Trist ran what came to be called a "Search Conference" to support a difficult merger. The new company was British aircraft engine company Bristol Siddeley. By the end of the session, the 11 top managers had "redefined the business they were in."[2]

Another seminal event occurred in the early 1980s when consultants Kathleen Dannemiller, Chuck Tyson, Alan Davenport, and Bruce Gibb brought together a 130-person management team, followed by nine additional management teams of comparable size, at Ford Motor Company. At the time, the optimal group size for addressing complex challenges was considered to be eight people. Few worked with more than 20 at a time. Ford sought breakthroughs in managing its businesses comparable to its breakthroughs in managing quality. Dannemiller and her partners involved the large groups, trusting the principle that having the whole system in the room was critical.

Through these five-day sessions, each management team "came to understand each other, the competition, and the market . . . as a coherent, energized, focused and aligned whole." They created strategic plans owned by all. They reorganized their structures and practices to support their goals, according to Nancy Badore, executive director of Ford Motor Company.[3]

What made these and other experiments distinct was (1) working with the whole system, and (2) involving the people of that system in finding their own answers. Two organizational development consultants noticed that something interesting was happening. Barbara Bunker and Billie Alban edited a 1992 special issue of the *Journal of Applied Behavioral Science* on this odd phenomenon. The issue told stories of using these emerging methodologies, calling them "large group interventions."[4] That journal issue catalyzed the field and accelerated the experimentation.

Since then, thousands of consultants and academics have used these change processes in organizations, communities, and other social systems around the world. They have improved businesses, cultivated communities, and influenced social systems like health care and education all over the world.

Brief descriptions of the processes referenced in this book follow. For more information on these and other processes that support the diverse people of a system to realize what matters to them, see *The Change Handbook*.[5]

Appreciative Inquiry

Appreciative Inquiry (AI) is based in asking possibility-oriented questions that focus on what is working and what is possible to inspire collaborative and wise action.[6]

Principles

CONSTRUCTIONIST PRINCIPLE—We construct realities based on our previous experience, so our knowledge and the destiny of the system are interwoven.

PRINCIPLE OF SIMULTANEITY—Inquiry and change are simultaneous.

POETIC PRINCIPLE—The system's story is constantly coauthored and is open to infinite interpretations.

ANTICIPATORY PRINCIPLE—What we anticipate determines what we find.

POSITIVE PRINCIPLE—As an image of reality is enhanced, actions begin to align with the positive image.

Phases of an AI Process

DISCOVERY—Mobilizing a multiple stakeholder inquiry into the positive core of a system.

DREAM—Creating a results-oriented vision based in discovered potential and questions of higher purpose, such as "What is the world calling us to become?"

DESIGN—Creating possibility-oriented design propositions of the ideal organization or community. Articulating a design capable of drawing upon and magnifying the positive core to realize the newly expressed dream.

DESTINY—Strengthening the affirmative capability of the whole system. Enabling it to build hope and sustain momentum for ongoing positive change and high performance.

At the center of this cycle is Affirmative Topic Choice. It is the starting point and most strategic aspect of any AI process. AI topics become an agenda for learning, knowledge sharing, and action. They get written into questions for Discovery interviews, and serve as seeds for Dreams, as arenas for crafting Design propositions, and for taking action in the Destiny phase.

Art of Hosting

Art of Hosting is a global community of practitioners using integrated participative change processes, methods, maps, and planning tools to engage groups and teams in meaningful conversation, deliberate collaboration, and group-supported action for the common good.[7]

Principles

High-quality conversation arises under the following conditions:

- People in a group are present and grounded, working with a common purpose.
- It is hosted in a container that invites participation and self-organization.
- People engage in participatory leadership, not top-down leadership, making the group's wisdom more available to itself.
- Groups working together over time act and harvest their learning through feedback loops that support action.

As Art of Hosting scales these generative principles up to larger and larger settings, the work becomes Art of Participatory Leadership. Rather than working with predetermined methods, the "art" is approaching each conversation from a design perspective, offering the best design for the context, based on simple principles.

Process

Art of Hosting is the "jazz" of emergent change processes. A team of hosts works with the conveners—often traditional leadership—to surface questions and activities that support their intentions for bringing people together. Hosting teams design the flow of an engagement by discerning what is most useful in the moment. Specific processes are often selected the evening before or the morning of an interaction. As hosting teams create the experience for participants, they invite the participants into the hosting itself. As a result, in addition to addressing the intended issue, participants are introduced to hosting skills. They learn how to ride the waves of the present moment while tending to an abiding intention.

Circle Process

Circle Process elicits deep speaking and listening that seems to arise from the form itself—a ring of chairs and a clearly defined purpose—inspiring collective wisdom and action.[8]

Principles and Practices

PeerSpirit Circling suggests three principles:

- Rotate leadership
- Share responsibility
- Rely on group synergy

And three practices:

- Speak intentionally
- Listen attentively
- Tend to the well-being of the group

Process

Circle begins by *setting the circle space*, including establishing a visual center that represents shared purpose or intention. A *check-in*—each person speaking briefly without comment or interruption—connects people, as they slow down and fully arrive. Often, a talking piece—an object that, when held, reminds the bearer to address the question and reminds everyone else to listen with curiosity—ensures that everyone has a chance to speak without interruption.

When coming together for the first time, circle participants discuss and *commit to group agreements*—often statements defining confidentiality, respectful interaction, and parameters of responsibility.

Someone volunteers to act as *host*, leading the topic from within the rim. And someone volunteers to serve as *guardian* of group time and energy. Within this framework, circle members move into the business or intention of the meeting, generally in a *free-flowing conversation*. When the subject is challenging, circle members may choose to reinstate the talking piece to slow the dialogue and stay in a mode of deep listening. Circle is brought to closure with a *check-out*— a talking-piece round to reflect on what has happened and harvest learning.

Dynamic Facilitation

Dynamic Facilitation (DF) helps individuals, groups, and large systems to address difficult, messy, or impossible-seeming issues, resulting in new possibilities, greater trust and collaboration, practical action steps, motivation, and exciting outcomes.[9, 10] It does this by stimulating a heartfelt creative quality of thinking called *choice-creating*, whereby people seek win-win breakthroughs.

Principles

- Creativity is key when facing complex or "impossible" issues.

- Diverse perspectives are essential for creative breakthroughs.

- Each person has a unique perspective and seeks to contribute to the larger whole, regardless of how he or she expresses it.

- Listening deeply to someone supports self-reflection and expression of meaning.

- When people can speak authentically and be heard, we discover our human connections.

- Creativity and authenticity flourish when protected from judgment.

- When diverse perspectives are held in a safe environment, we spontaneously create shared meanings and new, effective solutions that work for all.

Process

A Dynamic Facilitator encourages participants to work on high-care issues by speaking naturally and authentically about them. Instead of behavioral guidelines, preset agendas, or step-by-step procedures, DF's simple structure allows each contribution to be welcomed and heard even when the speaker might ordinarily be seen as disruptive. The facilitator's work is to "take all sides" and actively "protect" each person's contributions using four charts: data, solutions, concerns, and problem statements. He or she follows and supports participants' energy, welcoming even frustration or anger while eliciting desired hopes and wished-for outcomes. As the facilitator draws out each participant, reflecting back meaning and recording each contribution, shifts happen.

A series of sessions deepen personal changes, sustaining the new perspectives that emerge.

Future Search

Future Search, if the principles are followed, has the potential to transform an organization's or community's capability for action in one meeting.[11, 12] With "the whole system in the room," people generate a shared vision, an implementation plan, and high commitment to act—all in less than three days.

Principles

- Have the right people in the room—that is, a cross-section of the whole, including those who ARE IN: with *a*uthority, *r*esources, *e*xpertise, *i*nformation, and *n*eed.

- Create conditions where participants experience the whole "elephant" before acting on any part of it.

- Focus on the future and seek common ground rather than reworking problems and conflicts.

- Help people to take responsibility for their own conclusions and action plans.

Process

Five tasks occur in the approximate timeframes shown below.

Day 1 Afternoon

Task 1—Focus on the Past

Task 2—Focus on Present, External Trends

Day 2 Morning

Task 2 Continued—Stakeholder Response to External Trends

Task 2 Continued—Focus on Present, Owning Our Actions

Day 2 Afternoon

Task 3—Preferred Future Scenarios

Task 4—Identify Common Ground

Day 3 Morning

Task 4 Continued—Confirm Common Ground

Task 5—Action Planning

This task sequence is used successfully in cultures worldwide. People work entirely with their own experience. No diagnosis, vocabulary, or special inputs are required. People come together across lines of culture, class, education, age, gender, and ethnicity to create plans many once considered impossible. The method has been continuously tested and refined since 1982.

Open Space Technology

Open Space Technology invites people to self-organize by taking responsibility for what they love as a means to address complex, important issues.[13]

Principles and the Law

- Whoever comes are the right people.
- Whatever happens is the only thing that could have.
- When it starts is the right time.
- When it's over, it's over.

The Law of Two Feet (or, when being mindful of the disabled, the law of mobility) names the two fundamentals—the feet—on which Open Space runs: passion and responsibility. Passion engages the people in the room. Responsibility ensures that things get done.

An urgent theme or question focuses the event. The art of the question lies in saying just enough to evoke attention, while leaving sufficient open space for the imagination to run wild.

Process

All participants are seated in a circle (or concentric circles if the group is large). The principles and the law are introduced. Participants identify any issue for which they have some genuine passion and are prepared to take personal responsibility. They come to the center of the circle, write their issue on a piece of paper, announce it to the group, and post the paper on the wall. When all the issues have been surfaced, the participants go to the wall, sign up for the issues they care to deal with, and get to work. From there on out, the group is self-managing. As small groups meet, they generate reports. Participants come together at the end of each day to reflect and reach closure for the session.

Scenario Thinking

Scenario Thinking generates stories of alternative plausible futures to arrive at a deeper understanding in order to improve current and future decisions.[14]

A common approach to Scenario Thinking has five phases: orient, explore, synthesize, act, and monitor.

Phase One: Orient

Clarify the issue at stake by learning how challenges and underlying assumptions might play out in the future.

Phase Two: Explore

Determine the driving forces that could have an unexpected impact on the focal issue. Consider regulatory shifts or broader social, technological, economic, environmental, and political developments.

Phase Three: Synthesize

Identify the two or three most important and most uncertain driving forces. Picture these "critical uncertainties" on two axes. For instance, health care might cross uncertainty about the financial and regulatory environment with uncertainty about the pace and distribution of technological development. Envision the four scenarios created by this matrix: What if the financial and regulatory environments were favorable toward a freer market in health care, and technology developed and spread at a fast and even pace? This could be a world with a highly automated and efficient infrastructure for managing and administering health care with many choices and a weak safety net. Consider whether the possible scenarios produce believable and useful stories of the future.

Phase Four: Act

Use the scenarios to inform and inspire action. A good scenario set need not portray the future accurately. It supports learning, adaptation, and effective action.

Phase Five: Monitor

Track leading indicators—signs of emerging change. Is a particular scenario beginning to unfold, causing some implications to rise in importance and some uncertainties to evolve into certainties?

The World Café

The World Café fosters strategic dialogue by creating a living network of connected small-group conversations focused on shared "questions that matter" in order to foster the emergence of collective intelligence and committed action.[15]

Principles

When engaged as an integrated whole, these principles create the conditions that enable the "magic" of World Café dialogues to emerge and unfold:

- Set the context.
- Create hospitable space.
- Explore questions that matter.
- Encourage everyone's contribution.
- Cross-pollinate and connect diverse perspectives.
- Listen together for patterns, insights, and deeper questions.
- Harvest and share collective discoveries.

Process

Four people sit at a café-style table or in a small conversation cluster to explore a question or issue that matters to their life, work, or community. Other participants seated at nearby tables or in conversation clusters explore similar questions at the same time. As they talk, participants are encouraged to write down key ideas on large cards or to sketch them on paper tablecloths that are there for that purpose. After an initial 20- to 30-minute "round of conversation" in these intimate groups, participants are invited to change tables—carrying key ideas and insights from their previous conversation into the newly formed group. One "host" stays at each table to share with new arrivals the key images, insights, and questions that emerged from the prior dialogue. This process is repeated for several (generally three) rounds and is followed by a harvesting of the dialogue, to which all participants contribute.

NOTES

Preface

1. My notion of patterns comes from architect Christopher Alexander. Christopher Alexander, *The Timeless Way of Building* (New York: Oxford University Press, 1979); Christopher Alexander, Sara Ishikawa, and Murray Silverstein, *A Pattern Language: Towns, Buildings, Construction* (New York: Oxford University Press, 1977).
2. Peggy Holman and Tom Atlee, "Evolutionary Dynamics and Social Systems," *Integral Leadership Review* VIII, no. 2 (March 2008).

Introduction: From Chaos to Coherence

1. Bill Bishop, *The Big Sort: Why the Clustering of Like-Minded America Is Tearing Us Apart* (New York: Houghton Mifflin Harcourt, 2008).
2. Mark Fitzgerald and Jennifer Saba, "Special Report: Turn and Face the Change—With Newspaper Industry in Crisis, 'Everything's on the Table,'" *Editor and Publisher* (August 2008).
3. Erica Smith, "14,783+ jobs: 2009 layoffs and buyouts at U.S. newspapers," Paper Cuts, http://newspaperlayoffs.com/maps/2009-layoffs (accessed April 17, 2010).
4. Erica Smith, "Newspapers that have closed or stopped publishing a newsprint edition," Paper Cuts, http://newspaperlayoffs.com/maps/closed (accessed April 17, 2010).
5. Alan Deutschman, *Change or Die: The Three Keys to Change at Work and in Life* (New York: HarperBusiness, 2007).
6. Ibid.

Part I. The Nature of Emergence

1. Illustration by Steven Wright, steven@wrightmarks.com.

Chapter 1. What Is Emergence?

1. Steven Johnson, *Emergence: The Connected Lives of Ants, Brains, Cities, and Software* (New York: Scribner, 2001), 18.
2. Peter Corning, "The Re-emergence of 'Emergence': A Venerable Concept in Search of a Theory," *Complexity* 7, no. 6 (2002), 18–30.
3. Thomas Kuhn, *The Structure of Scientific Revolutions*, 3rd ed. (Chicago: University of Chicago Press, 1996), 85. While the phrase *paradigm shift* first appears on page 85, the whole of Kuhn's book describes the notion of transformation from one worldview to another.

4. M. Mitchell Waldrop, *Complexity: The Emerging Science at the Edge of Order and Chaos* (New York: Simon & Schuster, 1992), 67–77.
5. Ibid., p. 12.
6. Johnson, *Emergence*, 21.
7. Ibid.
8. Segment of network map. Reprinted by permission from the Govcom.org Foundation, Amsterdam (http://govcom.org). Thanks to Sheri Herndon for the idea and for catalyzing the mapping process. Thanks to Richard Rogers for creating the map. For the full map, visit www.newshare.com/wiki/images/7/76/GCO_Seattle_extended_large.pdf.

Chapter 2. What's the Catch?

1. David Bornstein, *How to Change the World: Social Entrepreneurs and the Power of New Ideas*, upd. ed. (New York: Oxford University Press, 2007). Referenced by Peter Block at Nexus for Change, Bowling Green, Ohio, 2008.
2. Green-Collar Jobs Campaign, www.ellabakercenter.org/index.php?p=gcjc_ green_jobs_ corps.
3. Michael Lombardi, "Century of Technology: 20 products that prove how Boeing made into reality what others dared to dream," January 2004, www .boeing.com/news/frontiers/archive/2003/december/cover1.html (accessed February 22, 2010).
4. "About JRMD/YRWD," www.jrmd.org/spip.php?article1 (accessed February 22, 2010).
5. The 900 followers of cult leader Jim Jones committed suicide by drinking grape Flavor Aid laced with cyanide at their commune in Jonestown, Guyana, in the late 1970s. Flavor Aid is an imitation of Kool-Aid.
6. *The State of the News Media 2004: An Annual Report on American Journalism*, Project for Excellence in Journalism, www.stateofthemedia.org/2004/narrative_ newspapers_audience.asp?cat=3&media=2.

Part II. Practices for Engaging Emergence

1. Illustration by Steven Wright, steven@wrightmarks.com.

Chapter 4. Prepare: Foster an Attitude for Engaging

1. Pema Chödrön, *The Places That Scare You: A Guide to Fearlessness in Difficult Times* (Boston: Shambhala Publications, 2007), 159.
2. David Gershon and Gail Straub, *Empowerment: The Art of Creating Your Life as You Want It* (New York: Dell Publishing, 1989), 12.
3. Mark Twain, *A Connecticut Yankee in King Arthur's Court* (New York: Harper & Brothers, 1917), 439.

Chapter 5. Host: Cultivate Conditions for Engaging

1. Michael Field and Martin Golubitsky, *Symmetry in Chaos: A Search for Pattern in Mathematics, Art, and Nature* (Oxford: Oxford University Press, 1992).
2. Peggy Holman, Tom Devane, and Steven Cady, *The Change Handbook: The Definitive Resource on Today's Best Methods for Engaging Whole Systems*, 2nd ed. (San Francisco: Berrett-Koehler Publishers, 2007), 44.
3. Marvin Weisbord and Sandra Janoff, *Future Search: An Action Guide to Finding Common Ground in Organizations and Communities*, 3rd ed. (San Francisco: Berrett-Koehler Publishers, 2010).

Chapter 6. Step In: Practice Engaging

1. Viktor Frankl, *Man's Search for Meaning*, rev. upd. ed. (New York: Pocket, 1997).
2. Marvin R. Weisbord, *Productive Workplaces: Organizing and Managing for Dignity, Meaning, and Community* (San Francisco: Jossey-Bass Publishers, 1987), 78–79.
3. *Book of Proceedings*, http://storyweavingthemes.pbworks.com/f/Book+of+Proceedings+FINAL+11-19-08pdf.pdf.
4. www.youtube.com/watch?v=6m7fpoAacBY&feature=related and www.youtube.com/watch?v=vRM1I90SOUw.
5. Image created with Wordle, www.wordle.net.
6. StoryWeavers, Welcome to Themefinding!, http://storyweavingthemes.pbworks.com (accessed February 21, 2010).

Chapter 7. Iterate: Do It Again . . . and Again

1. Michael Dowd, *Thank God for Evolution: How the Marriage of Science and Religion Will Transform Your Life and Our World* (New York: Viking, 2009).
2. Brian Swimme and Thomas Berry, *The Universe Story: From the Primordial Flaring Forth to the Ecozoic Era—A Celebration of the Unfolding of the Cosmos* (San Francisco: HarperSanFrancisco, 1992).
3. Donella H. Meadows, *Thinking in Systems: A Primer*, ed. Diana Wright (White River Junction, VT: Chelsea Green Publishing Co., 2008), 77, 78.

Part III. Principles for Engaging Emergence

1. Illustration by Steven Wright, steven@wrightmarks.com.

Chapter 9. Pioneer!

1. Apple, Inc. popularized "Think Different" in an ad campaign. A press release said they intended it "as a fanciful category, just as we might say 'Think

yellow,' 'Think change' or 'Think playful.'" Stephen Paul Gnass, "The People That Put On The Invention Convention®." Invention Convention, 2005, www.inventionconvention.com/grammar.html (accessed April 17, 2010).

Chapter 11. Seek Meaning

1. Andrew Sullivan, "The Revolution Will Be Twittered," *Daily Dish*, June 13, 2009, http://andrewsullivan.thatlantic.com/the_daily_dish/2009/06/the-revolution-will-be-twittered-1.html (accessed February 18, 2010).
2. This story is told in greater detail in Christina Baldwin and Ann Linnea, *The Circle Way: A Leader in Every Chair* (San Francisco: Berrett-Koehler Publishers, 2010), 169–75.

Chapter 12. Simplify

1. Adam Kahane, "Learning from Mont Fleur: Scenarios as a tool for discovering common ground," in Pieter le Roux, Vincent Maphai, et al., "The Mont Fleur Scenarios: What will South Africa be like in the year 2002?" *Deeper News* 7, no. 1 (Emeryville, CA: Global Business Network), 1–3, www.gbn .com/consulting/article_details.php?id=35&breadcrumb=ideas.
2. Adam Kahane, *Power and Love: A Theory and Practice of Social Change* (San Francisco: Berrett-Koehler Publishers, 2010).
3. Kahane, "Learning from Mont Fleur," 3.

Part IV. Three Questions for Engaging Emergence

1. Illustration by Steven Wright, steven@wrightmarks.com.

Chapter 15. How Do We Renew Coherence Wisely?

1. Elizabeth L. Eisenstein, *The Printing Press as an Agent of Change: Communications and Cultural Transformations in Early-Modern Europe* (New York: Cambridge University Press, 1979), 130.

In Closing: What's Possible Now?

1. Paul Hawken, *Blessed Unrest: How the Largest Social Movement in the World Came into Being and Why No One Saw It Coming* (New York: Viking, 2007).
2. Deborah Brandt, "The Be the Change Movement: An Emerging Beat?" (unpublished paper, Seattle, WA, March 2009).
3. From "Visible Earth," a catalog of NASA images, http://visibleearth.nasa.gov.
4. Joel de Rosnay, *The Symbiotic Man: A New Understanding of the Organization of Life and a Vision of the Future* (New York: McGraw-Hill, 2000).
5. Sunlight Foundation, 2010, http://sunlightfoundation.com (accessed February 16, 2010).
6. Robbie Schingler and Jessy Cowan-Sharp, OpenGov Tracker, February 2010, www.opengovtracker.com (accessed February 16, 2010).

7. Digg, digg labs, 2010, http://labs.digg.com (accessed February 16, 2010).
8. Minnesota Public Radio NewsQ, "Budget Balancer," 2007, http://minnesota
.publicradio.org/projects/2007/03/budget_balancer/ (accessed February 15, 2010).

About Emergent Change Processes

1. Barbara Benedict Bunker and Billie T. Alban, *Large Group Interventions: Engaging the Whole System for Rapid Change* (San Francisco: Jossey-Bass, 1997).
2. Marvin Ross Weisbord et al., *Discovering Common Ground: How Future Search Conferences Bring People Together to Achieve Breakthrough Innovation, Empowerment, Shared Vision, and Collaborative Action* (San Francisco: Berrett-Koehler Publishers, 1992).
3. Dannemiller Tyson Associates, *Whole-Scale Change Toolkit* (San Francisco: Berrett-Koehler Publishers, 2000).
4. Barbara Benedict Bunker and Billie T. Alban, eds. "Large Group Interventions" (special issue), *Journal of Applied Behavioral Science* 28, no. 4 (1992).
5. Holman et al., *The Change Handbook*, 2nd ed.
6. Diana Whitney and Amanda Trosten-Bloom, *The Power of Appreciative Inquiry: A Practical Guide to Positive Change* (San Francisco: Berrett-Koehler Publishers, 2003).
7. Art of Hosting, "A 4-fold way of hosting," February 15, 2010, www .artofhosting.org/theart/a4-foldway/ (accessed February 16, 2010).
8. Christina Baldwin and Ann Linnea, *The Circle Way: A Leader in Every Chair* (San Francisco: Berrett-Koehler Publishers, 2010).
9. Jim Rough and DeAnna Martin, "Dynamic Facilitation," in Peggy Holman, Tom Devane, and Steven Cady, *The Change Handbook*, 2nd ed.
10. Rosa Zubizarreta, "Practical Dialogue: Emergent Approaches for Effective Collaboration," in *Creating a Culture of Collaboration: The Interational Assocation of Facilitators Handbook*, ed. Sandy Schuman (San Francisco: Jossey-Bass, 2006).
11. Marvin Weisbord and Sandra Janoff, "Future Search: Common Ground Under Complex Conditions," in Holman et al., *The Change Handbook*, 2nd ed.
12. Weisbord and Janoff, *Future Search*.
13. Harrison Owen, *Open Space Technology: A User's Guide* (San Francisco: Berrett-Koehler Publishers, 1997).
14. Chris Ertel, Katherine Fulton, and Diana Scearce, "Scenario Thinking," in Holman et al., *The Change Handbook*, 2nd ed.
15. Juanita Brown, David Isaacs, and World Café Community, *The World Café: Shaping Our Futures Through Conversations That Matter* (San Francisco: Berrett-Koehler Publishers, 2005).

GLOSSARY

CHAOS—Disorder, confusion, random interaction among diverse agents.

COHERENCE/COALESCING—Coming together; converging into relationship, harmony, unity, bonding, community, shared sense, wholeness.

COMPASSION—The open-hearted capacity to enter into and be moved by our own and another's experience.

COMPLEXITY—Functional intricacy, especially the degree of diversity, connectivity, interdependence, and interaction involved in the self-organized functioning of a system.

CREATIVITY—The open-ended flow that brings novelty into being.

DIFFERENTIATION—Breaking apart; becoming separate; diverging, individuality, distinction, uniqueness.

DISRUPTION—Interruption of the status quo.

DISSONANCE—Lack of agreement or harmony; conflict.

DISTURBANCE—An emotionally troubling intrusion or interruption.

DIVERSITY—Variety, difference; the range of factors, such as race, class, gender, generation, geography, and function, to consider when engaging with a system.

EMERGENCE—Higher-order complexity arising out of chaos. Novel, coherent structures arising through interactions among diverse entities of a system.

EMERGENT CHANGE PROCESSES—Methods for engaging the diverse people of a system in focused yet open interactions that lead to unexpected and lasting shifts in perspective and behavior.

ENGAGEMENT—Participation, bringing the whole of oneself—head, heart, body, spirit.

FEEDBACK—Responses and reactions that give a system information about its interactions.

INTENTION—Purpose; implicit is a sense of calling, being guided by a deeper source of wisdom.

INTERACTION—Mutual or reciprocal action or influence.

INTUITION—Instinctive and unconscious knowing or sensing without deduction, reasoning, or using rational processes.

ITERATION—A repeating process in which the output of the current cycle becomes input to the next cycle.

LIFE ENERGY—Vitality, flow that attracts and enlivens, a nonphysical quality that animates all living organisms.

MACROSCOPE—A type of tool for sensing the infinitely complex; information, ideas, experiences, maps, stories, art, and media that help us to see ourselves in context.

PIONEER—To go before, to prepare or open a way. One who ventures into unknown or unclaimed territory. One who opens up new areas of thought, research, or development.

PRACTICE—A skill honed through continual study and experimentation. Discipline that develops both craft and artistry.

PRINCIPLE—A fundamental understanding or assumption that guides further understanding or action. Principles help us to find order out of chaos.

REFLECTION—(1) contemplation, consideration, search for meaning; (2) active mirroring of another's meaning—words, feelings, intentions.

RENEWAL—To make new again, with elements from the past and other elements that are original together forming something novel and of a higher-order complexity.

STRONG EMERGENCE—Higher-order complexity arising from interactions among diverse individual agents that is not deducible even in principle from the properties of the individual agents.

SUSTAINABILITY—The capacity of a system to maintain itself, to remain congruent with changing realities; resilience; the ability of a system to recover from disturbances and retain its essential identity, meeting its needs with attention to the ability of future generations to meet their needs.

SYSTEM—Interactions among diverse agents that persist and evolve as a coherent whole.

WEAK EMERGENCE—Higher-order complexity arising from interactions among diverse individual agents in which the essential properties are reasonably predictable but the specifics are unexpected (for example, we know it will be a baby but not its eye color, height, weight, etc.).

WISDOM—Knowledge or knowing that arises from and serves the whole; knowledge and knowing deeper than the rational mind; intuitions forged through experience.

BIBLIOGRAPHY

Alexander, Christopher. *The Timeless Way of Building*. New York: Oxford University Press, 1979.

Alexander, Christopher, Sara Ishikawa, and Murray Silverstein. *A Pattern Language: Towns, Buildings, Construction*. New York: Oxford University Press, 1977.

Art of Hosting. "A 4-fold way of Hosting." February 15, 2010. www .artofhosting.org/theart/a4-foldway/ (accessed February 16, 2010).

Atlee, Tom. *The Tao of Democracy: Using Co-Intelligence to Create a World That Works for All*. Cranston, RI: Writers' Collective, 2003.

Baldwin, Christina, and Ann Linnea. *The Circle Way: A Leader in Every Chair*. San Francisco: Berrett-Koehler Publishers, 2010.

Barlow, Connie. *Green Space, Green Time: The Way of Science*. New York: Springer-Verlag, 1997.

Bishop, Bill. *The Big Sort: Why the Clustering of Like-Minded America Is Tearing Us Apart*. New York: Houghton Mifflin Harcourt, 2008.

Bornstein, David. *How to Change the World: Social Entrepreneurs and the Power of New Ideas*. Upd. ed. New York: Oxford University Press, 2007.

Brandt, Deborah. *The Be the Change Movement: An Emerging Beat?* Seattle: Unpublished paper, March 2009.

Brown, Juanita, David Isaacs, and World Café Community. *The World Café: Shaping Our Futures Through Conversations That Matter*. San Francisco: Berrett-Koehler Publishers, 2005.

Bunker, Barbara Benedict, and Billie T. Alban, "Large Group Interventions" [Special Issue]. *Journal of Applied Behavioral Science* 28, no. 4 (1992).

———. *Large Group Interventions: Engaging the Whole System for Rapid Change*. San Francisco: Jossey-Bass, 1997.

Chödrön, Pema. *The Places That Scare You: A Guide to Fearlessness in Difficult Times*. Boston: Shambhala Publications, 2007.

Corning, Peter. "The Re-emergence of 'Emergence': A Venerable Concept in Search of a Theory." *Complexity* 7, no. 6 (2002): 18–30.

Dannemiller Tyson Associates. *Whole-Scale Change Toolkit*. San Francisco: Berrett-Koehler Publishers, 2000.

de Rosnay, Joel. *The Symbiotic Man: A New Understanding of the Organization of Life and a Vision of the Future*. New York: McGraw-Hill, 2000.

Deutschman, Alan. "Change or Die." *Fast Company.* May 1, 2005. www
.fastcompany.com/magazine/94/open_change-or-die.html (accessed July 25,
2009).

———. *Change or Die: The Three Keys to Change at Work and in Life.* New
York: HarperBusiness, 2007.

Digg. digg labs. 2010. http://labs.digg.com (accessed February 16, 2010).

Dowd, Michael. *Thank God for Evolution: How the Marriage of Science and
Religion Will Transform Your Life and Our World.* New York: Viking, 2009.

Eisenstein, Elizabeth L. *The Printing Press as an Agent of Change:
Communications and Cultural Transformations in Early-Modern Europe.*
New York: Cambridge University Press, 1979.

Field, Michael, and Martin Golubitsky. *Symmetry in Chaos: A Search for
Pattern in Mathematics, Art, and Nature.* Oxford: Oxford University Press,
1992.

Fitzgerald, Mark, and Jennifer Saba. "Special Report: Turn and Face the
Change—With Newspaper Industry in Crisis, 'Everything's on the Table.'"
Editor and Publisher (August 2008).

Frankl, Viktor E. *Man's Search for Meaning.* Rev. upd. ed. New York: Pocket,
1997.

Gershon, David, and Gail Straub. *Empowerment: The Art of Creating Your
Life as You Want It.* New York: Dell Publishing, 1989.

Girl Scouts of the USA. *Book of Proceedings,* 2008 National Council
Session 51st Convention. http://storyweavingthemes.pbworks.com/f/
Book+of+Proceedings+FINAL+11-19-08pdf.pdf.

Gnass, Stephen Paul. Invention Convention. *"The People That Put On The
Invention Convention®."* 2005. www.inventionconvention.com/grammar
.html (accessed 2010).

Green-Collar Jobs Campaign. 2009. www.ellabakercenter.org/index.php?
p=gcjc_green_jobs_corps (accessed 2009).

Hawken, Paul. *Blessed Unrest: How the Largest Movement in the World Came
into Being and Why No One Saw It Coming.* New York: Viking, 2007.

Holman, Peggy, and Tom Atlee. "Evolutionary Dynamics and Social Systems."
March 2008. www.integralleadershipreview.com/archives-2008/2008-
03/2008-03-article-holman-atlee.php.

Holman, Peggy, and Tom Devane. *The Change Handbook: Group Methods
for Shaping the Future.* San Francisco: Berrett-Koehler Publishers, 1999.

Holman, Peggy, Tom Devane, and Steven Cady. *The Change Handbook: The
Definitive Resource on Today's Best Methods for Engaging Whole Systems.*
2nd ed. San Francisco: Berrett-Koehler Publishers, 2007.

Johnson, Steven. *Emergence: The Connected Lives of Ants, Brains, Cities, and Software.* New York: Scribner, 2001.

Journalism That Matters. *Journalism That Matters, Pacific Northwest.* January 2010. www.newshare.com/wiki/images/7/76/GCO_Seattle_ extended_large.pdf (accessed February 22, 2010).

JRMD/YRWD. "About JRMD/YRWD." www.jrmd.org/spip.php?article1 (accessed February 22, 2010).

Kahane, Adam. "Learning from Mont Fleur: Scenarios as a Tool for Discovering Common Ground." In Pieter le Roux, Vincent Maphai, et al., "The Mont Fleur Scenarios: What will South Africa be like in the year 2002?" Global Business Network. *Deeper News* 7, no. 1. www.gbn.com/ consulting/article_details.php?id=35&breadcrumb=ideas (accessed 2009).

———. *Power and Love: A Theory and Practice of Social Change.* San Francisco: Berrett-Koehler Publishers, 2010.

Kauffman, Stuart. *At Home in the Universe: The Search for the Laws of Self-Organization and Complexity.* New York: Oxford University Press, 1996.

Kuhn, Thomas. *The Structure of Scientific Revolutions.* Chicago: University of Chicago Press, 1962.

Liota, Vincent (producer and editor). "Emergence." *NOVA scienceNOW.* July 10, 2007. Boston: WGBH. www.pbs.org/wgbh/nova/sciencenow/3410/03.html.

Lombardi, Michael. "Century of Technology: 20 products that prove how Boeing made into reality what others dared to dream." January 2004. www .boeing.com/news/frontiers/archive/2003/december/cover1.html (accessed February 22, 2010).

Meadows, Donella H. *Thinking in Systems: A Primer.* Diana Wright, ed. White River Junction, VT: Chelsea Green Publishing Co., 2008.

Minnesota Public Radio. "Budget Balancer." 2007. http://minnesota .publicradio.org/projects/2007/03/budget_balancer/ (accessed February 15, 2010).

Owen, Harrison. *Open Space Technology: A User's Guide.* San Francisco: Berrett-Koehler Publishers, 1997.

Project for Excellence in Journalism. *The State of the News Media 2004: An Annual Report on American Journalism.* 2004. www.stateofthemedia .org/2004/narrative_newspapers_audience.asp?cat=3&media=2 (accessed 2009).

Schingler, Robbie, and Jessy Cowan-Sharp. *OpenGov Tracker.* February 2010. www.opengovtracker.com/ (accessed February 16, 2010).

Smith, Erica. "14,783+ jobs: 2009 layoffs and buyouts at U.S. newspapers." Paper Cuts. http://newspaperlayoffs.com/maps/2009-layoffs (accessed April 17, 2010).

———. "Newspapers that have closed or stopped publishing a newsprint edition." Paper Cuts. http://newspaperlayoffs.com/maps/closed (accessed April 17, 2010).

StoryWeavers. "Welcome to Themefinding!" StoryWeaving Themes. http://storyweavingthemes.pbworks.com (accessed February 21, 2010).

Sullivan, Andrew. *The Revolution Will Be Twittered.* June 13, 2009. http://andrewsullivan.theatlantic.com/the_daily_dish/2009/06/the-revolution-will-be-twittered-1.html (accessed February 18, 2010).

Sunlight Foundation. 2010. http://sunlightfoundation.com (accessed February 16, 2010).

Swimme, Brian, and Thomas Berry. *The Universe Story: From the Primordial Flaring Forth to the Ecozoic Era—A Celebration of the Unfolding of the Cosmos.* San Francisco: HarperSanFrancisco, 1992.

Waldrop, M. Mitchell. *Complexity: The Emerging Science at the Edge of Chaos.* New York: Simon and Schuster, 1992.

Weisbord, Marvin R. *Productive Workplaces: Organizing and Managing for Dignity, Meaning, and Community.* San Francisco: Jossey-Bass, 1987.

Weisbord, Marvin R., et al. *Discovering Common Ground: How Future Search Conferences Bring People Together to Achieve Breakthrough Innovation, Empowerment, Shared Vision, and Collaborative Action.* San Francisco: Berrett-Koehler Publishers, 1992.

Weisbord, Marvin R., and Sandra Janoff. *Future Search: Getting the Whole System in the Room for Vision, Commitment, and Action,* 3rd ed. San Francisco: Berrett-Koehler Publishers, 2010.

Wheatley, Margaret J. *Leadership and the New Science: Learning about Organization from an Orderly Universe.* San Francisco: Berrett-Koehler Publishers, 1992.

Whitney, Diana, and Amanda Trosten-Bloom. *The Power of Appreciative Inquiry: A Practical Guide to Positive Change.* San Francisco: Berrett-Koehler Publishers, 2003.

World Café. "What Is World Café?" www.youtube.com/watch?v=6m7fpoAac BY&feature=related. "Seven Principles of World Café." www.youtube.com/watch?v=vRM1I90SOUw.

Zubizarreta, Rosa. "Practical Dialogue: Emergent Approaches for Effective Collaboration." In *Creating a Culture of Collaboration: The International Assocation of Facilitators Handbook,* edited by Sandy Schuman. San Francisco: Jossey-Bass, 2006.

ACKNOWLEDGMENTS

Thus we have each of us cause to think
with deep gratitude of those who have
lighted the flames within us.

—Albert Schweitzer, *Memoirs of Childhood*
   and Youth

Books exist because of the kindness, challenge, and support that authors receive from people and circumstances around them. I thank the colleagues who contributed illustrations and stories; the people who gave me feedback on the manuscript; the thought leaders, teachers, and learning partners who influenced me; the artists who worked with me to make abstract ideas visual; the editorial and production support people at Berrett-Koehler; and the friends who helped in a variety of unexpected ways.

To Steven Wright, thank you for your great eye and fabulous illustrations. Working with you is a treat!

For writing stories, I thank Christina Baldwin, Juanita Brown, Sandra Janoff, Mark Jones, Adam Kahane, DeAnna Martin, Heather Tischbein, Christine Whitney Sanchez, and Tenneson Woolf.

To the patient readers who found gold and took the time to help me mine it, thank you: Tom Atlee, Sherri Black, Deborah Brandt, Tree Bressen, Tree Fitzpatrick, Jill Geisler, Sandra Janoff, Gail Koelln, DeAnna Martin, Magi Oriah Nock, Larry Peterson, Lori Rosolowsky, Martin Rutte, Nancy White, and Rosa Zubizarreta.

To others who commented on some aspect of the manuscript, shared in a story, or both, you have my gratitude: Bill Aal, Andrés Agudelo, Jennifer Atlee, Tova Averbuch, Emily Axelrod, Azalea Blalock, Peter Block, Phillip Bonser, Frank Catanzaro, Chris Corrigan,

Scott Davis, Tom Devane, Michael Dowd, Howard Finberg, Katherine
Fulton, Sono Hashisaki, Seth Henry, Jon Host, Christopher Innes,
Lion Goodman, Sylvia James, Van Jones, Lion Kimbro, Amy Lenzo,
Nancy Margulies, Holger Nauheimer, Dan Oestreich, Manuel Ortega,
Geneva Overholser, Harrison Owen, Sabine Pannwitz, Jessica Partnow,
Gifford Pinchot, Libba Pinchot, Cathy Remus, Martin Reynolds, Peter
Rinearson, Diane Robbins, Kelly Robson, Alberto Rossi, Jim Rough,
Pankaj Sapkal, Stephen Silha, Maurreen Skowran, Anne Stadler,
Sarah Stuteville, Samantha Tan, Gail Taylor, Penny Walker, and Leslye
Wood.

To Steve Cady, thanks for pulling together a group to review the
book with me in real time: Sherri Black, Kristoff Koch, Emily Lewis,
DeAnna Martin, Nancy McMorrow, and Lizette Tucker. What an intense and valuable process!

My thanks to Connie Barlow for reviewing the science. Any errors
remaining are mine.

To the Berrett-Koehler reviewers, no question the book is better because of your counsel: Katherine Armstrong, Frances Baldwin, Marisa
Handler, Jeff Kulick, and Rebecca Maillet. In particular, Katherine,
your mixture of enthusiasm and challenging, specific advice guided
me closely as I rewrote. If it is a friendlier, more accessible book, you
are a big part of why.

To Diana Whitney, who told me in 2008, "Peggy, you need to
write a book": Diana, you were right! And for encouraging me to
take the plunge as I put my toe in the waters of these ideas, thank you,
Peter Block.

The ideas I share have many influences. While I never knew three
of my teachers—Thomas Kuhn, Christopher Alexander, and Thomas
Berry—many of the thought leaders who have influenced me I'm glad
to call friends. My thanks to Billie Alban, Dick and Emily Axelrod,
Juanita Brown, Barbara Bunker, David Cooperrider, Sandra Janoff,
Harrison Owen, Jim Rough, Brian Swimme, Marvin Weisbord, Meg
Wheatley, and Diana Whitney.

Deep gratitude to my fellow travelers in learning what it means to engage emergence: Tova Averbuch, Connie Barlow, Chris Corrigan, Michael Dowd, Tree Fitzpatrick, Candi Foon, Teresa Posakony, Christine Whitney Sanchez, and Tenneson Woolf. In particular, Anne Stadler, Mark Jones, and Tom Atlee, you have been constant companions. So many ideas are rooted in our conversations and experiences together.

To my Journalism That Matters partners, it's been quite a road! Our work taught me about the challenging realities of emergence. Many thanks to Stephen Silha, for your partnership. To our companions, Chris Peck, Bill Densmore, and Cole Campbell (deceased but not forgotten), we couldn't have done it without you.

To the staff at Berrett-Koehler, you sure know how to support an author! My thanks to Jeevan Sivasubramaniam, Steve Piersanti, and especially my editor, Johanna Vondeling. Johanna, your confidence in me gave me confidence. Elissa Rabellino, your gracious, rigorous copyediting adds accuracy and polish. It also keeps me humble. Thank you. Linda Jupiter and team, thank you for a beautiful design.

Teresa Posakony and Steven Donaldson: your place at Ocean Shores held me, giving me the spaciousness to focus and write. Paul Dupree: thank you for your design sensibilities. Images of people made it in! Sheri Herndon and Richard Rogers, thank you for the network map. Kathy Ryan, thank you for the shared learning during our morning walks. Shelley Schermer, many thanks for your design eye on the book cover. Guillermina Hernandez-Gallegos, my gratitude to you for, on behalf of the W. K. Kellogg Foundation, funding research on evolutionary dynamics that can be used to transform social systems. That work provided seminal insights for this book.

Finally, I thank my husband, Neil, for so many reasons! Among them: sounding board, cheerleader, and chief nudger. Thank you for being patient every time I disappeared into a writing haze. I love you.

INDEX

ABOUT THE AUTHOR

Photo by Kris Krug

I've always been happiest when I'm learning, especially when it engages both my head and my heart. That may explain how I ended up with an undergraduate degree in drama and an MBA with an emphasis in finance.

I spent the first 17 years of my working life in software. I was a programmer, project manager, and systems development manager. In 1993, I ran into emergent change processes. Working with processes and people appealed to the part of me that found software wasn't enough. After experimenting with these processes in corporate settings, in 1996 I left organizational life to consult and pursue my quest to understand what made emergent change processes effective.

That first foray led to *The Change Handbook* (1999), coedited with Tom Devane. The book, considered the "bible" for the field, provided 18 methodologies for engaging whole systems.

In addition to corporate clients, my consulting practice attracted government agencies and nonprofits that wanted to engage civil society to find answers to complex questions.

In 2001, I joined three journalists to cofound Journalism That Matters. We bring together pioneers in the throes of emergence, as providing news and information experiences a death and rebirth. Working with such upheaval requires both head and heart!

In 2004, with social philosopher Tom Atlee and "evolutionary evangelist" Michael Dowd, I cohosted an "Evolutionary Salon"—a gathering of scientists, spiritual leaders, and social activists to explore the implications of evolutionary emergence for human systems. After four salons, the W. K. Kellogg Foundation funded Tom and me in developing a model of evolution centered on the role of interaction. It deepened my understanding of emergence and convinced me that there was something important to share.

Steven Cady joined Tom Devane and me to create the vastly revised 2007 edition of *The Change Handbook*. Because the field has exploded, the book included over 60 methodologies. That growth inspired me to dive into the deeper patterns of these methods and connect them with a theory of emergence to create the book you now hold.

● ● ●

Peggy Holman lives in Bellevue, Washington, with her husband. You can visit her at www.peggyholman.com.

Peggy Holman, Tom Devane, and Steven Cady,
with over 90 International Contributors

The Change Handbook
**The Definitive Resource on Today's Best Methods
for Engaging Whole Systems**

This extensively updated second edition of the classic bestseller features profiles of sixty-one change methods by the originators and foremost practitioners of such high-leverage change methods as Appreciative Inquiry, the World Café, Six Sigma, Future Search, and Open Space Technology. The authors outline distinctive aspects of their approach, answer frequently asked questions, and provide case studies and references to learn more. A one-stop comparative chart helps you determine which methods will work best for you, along with chapters on mixing and matching and sustaining results. This tremendously expanded second edition is the definitive resource in the exciting area of engaging "whole systems" of people to create their own future.

Paperback, 752 pages, ISBN 978-1-57675-379-8
PDF ebook, ISBN 978-1-57675-509-9

Berrett–Koehler Publishers, Inc.
www.bkconnection.com   **800.929.2929**

Berrett–Koehler
Publishers

A community dedicated to creating
a world that works for all

Visit Our Website: www.bkconnection.com

Read book excerpts, see author videos and Internet movies, read our
authors' blogs, join discussion groups, download book apps, find out about
the BK Affiliate Network, browse subject-area libraries of books, get special
discounts, and more!

Subscribe to Our Free E-Newsletter, the *BK Communiqué*

Be the first to hear about new publications, special discount offers, exclu-
sive articles, news about bestsellers, and more! Get on the list for our free
e-newsletter by going to **www.bkconnection.com.**

Get Quantity Discounts

Berrett-Koehler books are available at quantity discounts for orders of ten or
more copies. Please call us toll-free at (800) 929-2929 or email us at **bkp
.orders@aidcvt.com.**

Join the BK Community

BKcommunity.com is a virtual meeting place where people from around
the world can engage with kindred spirits to create a world that works for
all. **BKcommunity.com** members may create their own profiles, blog, start
and participate in forums and discussion groups, post photos and videos,
answer surveys, announce and register for upcoming events, and chat with
others online in real time. Please join the conversation!

MIX
Paper from
responsible sources

FSC
www.fsc.org **FSC® C012752**